OTHELLO

OTHELLO

OTHELLO

WILLIAM SHAKESPEARE

INTRODUCTION
BY DR CHRIS MCNAB

This edition published in 2023 by Arcturus Publishing Limited
26/27 Bickels Yard, 151–153 Bermondsey Street,
London SE1 3HA

Typesetting by Sooky Choi

Cover design: Peter Ridley
Cover illustration: Paula Zamudio

AD010245UK

Printed in the UK

CONTENTS

INTRODUCTION 7

DRAMATIS PERSONÆ 32

OTHELLO 33

GLOSSARY 149

NOTES 169

WILLIAM SHAKESPEARE –
HIS LIFE AND TIMES 182

INTRODUCTION

Honesty. That word thumps like a drumbeat throughout *Othello: honest* appears 42 times, and *honesty* nine times. The word is so loaded because honesty is emphatically not what Shakespeare presents in this powerful drama. Instead, the audience is witness to a tortuous web of deceit, suspicion, villainy, amorality and slander, most formulated through the skilful machinations of the individual who is arguably Shakespeare's purest villain, Iago. The fact that others attach the honest label so frequently to Iago makes the play painful to the audience, as from the outset we see that his *honesty* is just a mask for evil designs. Doubling the tension is the fact that Iago's motives are not transparent, giving his evil a hint of randomness that amplifies the horror of what occurs.

SOURCES AND CONTEXT

In the writing of *Othello* Shakespeare drew on one principal source, the *Hecatommithi* by Giovanni Battista Giraldi (1504–73), an Italian novelist and poet often known by his nickname Cinthio (or Cinzio), whose work was a reference not only for *Othello* but also *Measure for Measure*. Giraldi tells the story of the Moor and his wife Disdemona in Venice, their marital bliss progressively wrecked by the Moor's Ensign (a junior commissioned officer rank). The Ensign falls in love with Disdemona, and persuades the Moor that she has been unfaithful with Cassio. Together they plot her murder, although in the *Hecatommithi* it is the Ensign who does the deed, beating Disdemona to death with a stocking filled with sand, then bringing down a ceiling on her to conceal the killing, unsuccessfully. Ultimately, the Moor is exiled and killed by Disdemona's relatives, while the Ensign eventually ends his life under torture in prison.

Shakespeare made some significant adaptive changes to this core plot, including altering the nature of Iago's motivation, introducing new characters such as Roderigo and Brabantio, and setting the play in the war between the Turks and the Venetians, splitting the action between Venice and Cyprus.

Some wider historical context is useful here, and has a bearing on how we interpret *Othello*. From its origins in the seventh century in what is now Saudi Arabia, Islam underwent a long period of formidable military expansion, eventually threatening Christian (Catholic) Europe. In the eighth century, the Iberian Peninsula (Spain and Portugal) fell, although European forces would eventually claw it back between the eleventh and fifteenth centuries. From the fourteenth century, Europe was also in an intermittent state of war with the Muslim Ottoman Turkish empire, which expanded out from the Middle East and North Africa into south-eastern Europe. Cyprus was a key Christian outpost in the Mediterranean, a Venetian colony from 1489 to 1571. The action in *Othello* takes place in the last two years of this period.

Setting *Othello* in Cyprus and Venice, during a time of war between Islam and Christianity, allowed Shakespeare to tap into English associations about two very different worlds. To the Jacobean audience (the first recorded performance of *Othello* was in 1604, one year after the death of Elizabeth I, with a new king, James I of England and Ireland and VI of Scotland, on the throne), Venice was commercial, cosmopolitan and wealthy, class-conscious but also meritocratic. It was a major centre of maritime trade between Europe and the East, meaning that the humming, busy city was a melting-pot culture of many foreigners. Othello is one of them – a mercenary in Venetian hire, a common practice at the time. Wider Italy was regarded with some ambivalence in England, renowned for its culture, learning and urbanity, but also for hidden licentiousness and corruption.

The label 'Moor' was used as a blanket term by Europeans to denote Muslim inhabitants of the Iberian Peninsula, Sicily and Malta, as well as North Africa. Othello, however, is a Christianized Moor. His switch of faith would not have removed him entirely from Renaissance suspicions. In wider Renaissance drama, Moors were sometimes figures of uncertain threat, treading the line between the perceived barbarity of the heathen and the civilization of the Europeans. Romantic relations between black men and white women held a special horror, cemented by the belief that the offspring would somehow be monstrous.

In contrast to Venice, Cyprus signified threat, straddling the fault lines between East and West. The storm that opens Act II isolates the island dramatically, as does the circling danger of the Turks. It is a martial island of fortifications and defences, a conceptual border zone beyond the normal world and the other. But choosing Cyprus as a setting was also a canny and flattering nod towards the patron of Shakespeare's acting company, the King's Men – none other than the new monarch, James. The king was a keen student of the Ottoman–Christian Wars, and had even written a poem about the battle of Lepanto in 1571, when a Christian league destroyed the Ottoman fleet in a famous clash in the Ionian Sea

By setting much of the action in Cyprus, Shakespeare placed the audience for *Othello* at the confluence of contrasting cultural rivers. The skill inherent in the play is that Shakespeare makes the navigation of these waters – racially, psychologically, socially, sexually – inherently challenging and fascinating.

PLOT SUMMARY AND COMMENTARY

In **Act I, scene i**, on the night-time streets of Venice, we meet Iago, ensign to Othello the Moor. Iago talks with Roderigo, a weak gentleman in thrall to Iago's bullish character. Roderigo is at first complaining that Iago is controlling his money without explaining his actions or purpose. Iago deftly provides more context. He reveals that Othello has promoted one Michael Cassio to be his deputy, a position that Iago expected. Iago views Cassio disparagingly as a 'Florentine' (I. i. 20) – in other words, an outsider – and a mere theoretician without proper military experience. He explains that he will have his revenge but will hide his real intentions behind a mask of obedience: "I follow him to serve my turn upon him" (I. i. 42).

The first step of Iago's plan is executed immediately. The two men go to the house of Brabantio, a Venetian senator and father of Desdemona, a young woman for whom Roderigo has romantic desires. Standing outside, Iago shouts out that Brabantio's house has been robbed and Desdemona has been taken by an 'old black ram' (I. i. 88) for sex. He adds fuel to the growing blaze by naming Othello, while hiding his own identity in the shadows:

> I am one, sir, that comes to tell you your
> daughter and the Moor are now making the
> beast with two backs.

I. i. 116–118

Brabantio is roused, and recognizes Roderigo, who elaborates further on the background of the illicit romance. Brabantio and his staff search the house and confirm that Desdemona is indeed missing. He fears that she has been bewitched by Othello with dark magic, and he raises a party to hunt for her.

The first scene sets the manipulative skill of Iago, dangling Roderigo like a puppet-master controlling the wires of his toy. At this point, Othello is only viewed through the prism of others, the language of his description infused with racial contempt.

In **Act I, scene ii**, Iago makes one of the deft switches of position that will characterize his dramatic influence over the play. He strides onto the stage with Othello, the central character now given the opportunity to reveal himself directly to the audience. Stacking his lies, Iago tells Othello that Roderigo has been slandering him and that Brabantio is on the warpath. Othello, projecting authority, feels that his redoubtable military career and personal bearing will put the situation right.

In a sudden interjection, Cassio enters with a message, bringing news about a military emergency occurring in Cyprus, a threat that requires Othello's presence at the Venetian Council. Iago hurriedly informs Cassio that Othello has secretly wed – but doesn't get a chance to say to whom before Brabantio bursts into the scene. Swords are drawn and the tension is high, but Othello attempts to calm the situation. Brabantio accuses Othello of bewitching Desdemona; Othello reacts with noble restraint, and the two men agree to present their cases to the Duke. In this scene, Othello undoubtedly projects the bearing and authority of the military commander, but there is also the suggestion of his character moderated and calmed by marriage.

Act II, scene iii opens in the Venetian Council chamber, with the Duke and senators in attendance. Discussion centres around reports that an Ottoman Turk invasion fleet is bound for Cyprus. The conference is disrupted by the arrival of Brabantio, Othello, Iago, Roderigo and attendants. Brabantio lays out his accusations against Othello for the Duke, before Othello steps up to defend himself. He explains that he is indeed married to Desdemona, and explains how he will recount how this came about in the straightforward language of a soldier, recognizing that his manners have been crafted in battle and therefore his speech is not suited to the 'soft phrase of peace' (I. iii. 82). His speech is a mix of prose and blank verse, defining his authenticity amid the frequent poetic courtly language. He details how he won Desdemona's heart through a natural evolution of fondness between the two, attracting her through his character, history and gentle interactions.

The Duke is convinced, his view further cemented when Desdemona enters and confirms Othello's story, making her own declaration of dutiful love. She reveals herself as self-possessed and clear-sighted, fully at the helm of her actions. Brabantio, reluctantly, concedes the legitimacy of the romance. But affairs of state intervene – Othello will be pulled between domesticity and conflict, mirroring the internal struggle between tenderness and violence. The Duke orders Othello to go to Cyprus to take command of the island's defences. After discussion, it is agreed that Desdemona will go with him – the depth of their love bars separation – although Othello reassures the Duke that the distractions of love will not compromise his leadership. The Duke orders preparations for the journey, with Desdemona, in the predatory care of Iago, sailing on a different ship to her husband.

All now exit except Iago and Roderigo. The latter is tormented by Othello's marriage to Desdemona, but Iago mocks him for being so emasculated and sensitive, decrying virtue itself and scorning suicide as an attempted escape route from the torments of passion. Iago reassures Roderigo that he will help him in his quest to claim Desdemona, albeit on condition of payment. Iago punctuates his explanation with weirdly insistent phrases about the need for Roderigo to pay up for his help, the point hammered home almost hypnotically. At the same time, he reveals his true feelings (at least 'true' to his actions) for Othello and Desdemona:

> Make all the money thou canst:
> if sanctimony and a frail vow betwixt an erring
> barbarian and a supersubtle Venetian be not too
> hard for my wits and all the tribe of hell, thou
> shalt enjoy her; therefore make money.

I. iii. 361–365

Roderigo is again caught on the hook. He will follow Desdemona to Cyprus, where Iago says he will engineer circumstances to their advantage. Roderigo leaves, giving Iago the freedom to confess his joyous exploitation of gullible individuals like Roderigo. Notably, he also hints at rumours that Othello has actually slept with Iago's wife, Emilia. It is unclear how sincerely this is believed, or is it simply a device to reinforce his own malign will? He plots to raise suspicion of an affair between Cassio and Desdemona, relying on Othello's own honest nature and new-found happiness to whip up darker impulses.

Act II, scene i moves the action to Cyprus. Montano, the former governor of the island, is in awed discussion with some gentlemen, together describing the cataclysmic storm offshore. They celebrate the fact that it has wrecked and scattered the Turkish invasion fleet, but at the same time the storm feels like an ill portent given that Othello, his wife, Cassio and Iago are riding the same seas. The conversation focuses on the incoming parties. The Third Gentleman shares information that Cassio's ship has safely arrived, while the Fourth Gentleman announces the arrival of another ship, later revealed to be carrying Desdemona and Iago. Cassio enters, reassuring the group of the seaworthiness of Othello's vessel and informing them of their new commander's marriage.

Desdemona and Iago now enter. Cassio rapturously hails Desdemona, but the lady is more concerned about Othello's whereabouts. There is relief as another sail is spotted at sea – Othello has arrived. Prior to his entering the scene, Desdemona and Emilia (who has also come to Cyprus) engage in a bawdy, joking interchange with Iago, a verbal battle over the qualities of women in which Iago's misogyny is mediated with humour. Iago proves his wit in the nimble wordplay, but his asides chill the mood for the audience, who realize that all his interactions are in fact so many moves on a malevolent chessboard, such as when Cassio innocently takes Desdemona's hand:

> He takes her by the palm: ay, well said,
> whisper: with as little a web as this will I
> ensnare as great a fly as Cassio

II. i. 168–170

Eventually Othello steps onto the stage, enthralled to be reunited with Desdemona while also celebrating the destruction of the Ottoman fleet. But when all but Iago and Roderigo exit, Iago keeps the plates spinning. To Roderigo he fabricates a claim that Desdemona is actually in love with Cassio. He feeds Roderigo's incredulous nature, not with facts but rather with universal observations that fuel paranoia and suspicion. Iago also unleashes a racial character assassination of Othello.

The first step of Iago's plan is revealed. He will get Roderigo to incite Cassio to violence, resulting in Cassio's dismissal from Othello's service. Roderigo buys into the plan and exits. Alone, Iago reveals some of the deeper motivations for his actions, including his own lust for Desdemona and, again, the possibility that Othello has cuckolded him:

> Now, I do love her too,
> Not out of absolute lust, though peradventure
> I stand accountant for as great a sin,
> But partly led to diet my revenge,
> For that I do suspect the lusty Moor
> Hath leap'd into my seat

II. i. 300–305

Again, the degree to which this is truly believed is uncertain – Iago might simply be whipping himself into action imaginatively (see the more detailed character analysis of Iago below).

Act II, scene ii, is extremely brief – a Herald enters and announces the destruction of the Turkish fleet and that Othello has proclaimed a day of general festivities and revelry, in part also to celebrate his marriage to Desdemona. **Act II, scene iii** sees Iago's machinations start to gain traction. Cassio has been given oversight of the celebrations, to ensure they stay within respectable limits. Othello retires with Desdemona, leaving Iago and Cassio in dialogue. Iago attempts to draw Cassio into salacious observations regarding Desdemona, although Cassio persistently counters with respectful praise. Iago proceeds to get Cassio drunk against his wishes, knowing that the drink will loosen his bonds of self-control. During this scene, Iago is full of bawdy song and high spirits, manipulating those around with his intoxicating energy and quick wit.

Eventually Cassio leaves and Iago talks reprovingly with Montano, hinting that Cassio is a drunk. To the side, Iago sends Roderigo to intercept Cassio and provoke a chase and fight. The plan works to perfection. Cassio enters, roaring angrily and chasing Roderigo, but ending up in a fight in which Cassio wounds Montano. Iago plays the part of mediator brilliantly, but Othello is summoned, his marital night interrupted by the fracas. Othello speaks powerfully and harshly about what he sees, but turns to Iago for insight, showing his dependency upon this corrupting figure. Iago affects innocence and neutrality, and Othello rebukes Cassio and Montano, giving us the opportunity to see his anger unleashed. Iago manipulates the narrative of the events and Othello's instincts, leading to the point where Othello sacks Cassio from his position as deputy.

Desdemona briefly appears on stage before she retires with Othello. Iago and a mortified Cassio remain. Cassio laments the destruction of his reputation, but Iago comforts him by insisting that Othello's rage will pass, stacking up more layers of character-driven irony. To help Cassio's case, Iago suggests that Cassio should appear to Desdemona as an influential intermediary. Cassio agrees and leaves. Iago delivers a soliloquy in which, in effect, he defends himself to a hostile audience:

> And what's he then that says I play the villain?
> When this advice is free I give and honest,
> Probal to thinking, and indeed the course
> To win the Moor again?

> II. iii. 342–345

Here Iago appears to suggest that he is a fair broker, but by the end of the soliloquy his intentions are openly poisonous:

> And she for him pleads strongly to the Moor,
> I'll pour this pestilence into his ear,
> That she repeals him for her body's lust

> II. iii. 361–363

The scene ends when Roderigo enters, clearly despondent at having spent all his money for fruitless outcomes. Iago convinces him to have patience. When Roderigo leaves, Iago outlines his plan to have Emilia pressurize Desdemona to intercede on Cassio's behalf, while Iago crafts an opportunity for Othello to witness Cassio pleading with Desdemona.

Cassio is the opening focus of **Act III, scene i**. He has hired some musicians to entertain Othello, but the Clown mocks their musical ability and dismisses them. It is another, albeit minor, illustration of how easily Cassio is overruled. He then asks the Clown to send Emilia to him. In the meantime, Iago enters, reassuring Cassio that he will choreograph a reconciliation. Emila enters and says that she is conferring with Desdemona, who in turn is making representations to Othello. Cassio, however, wants to speak with Desdemona alone.

Act III, scene ii is a brief episode in which Othello gives Iago letters to take to the pilot of a ship, to deliver to Venice, then announces he will inspect the island's fortifications. Although short, the scene reminds us that Othello's presence in Cyprus is a military deployment, and Iago's behind-the-scenes plotting will indeed lead to the type of distractions which Othello promised the Council would not be a problem.

Act III, scene iii is pivotal. It opens with Desdemona, Emilia and Cassio in discussion, with Desdemona reassuring Cassio of the eventual restoration of relations with Othello. Othello and Iago then enter. Cassio leaves, embarrassed, despite Desdemona telling him to stay. Iago seizes on the awkwardness to plant the first seeds of suspicion in Othello's mind:

> *Oth.*   Was not that Cassio parted from my wife?
> *Iago.* Cassio, my lord! No, sure, I cannot think it.
>   That he would steal away so guilty-like,
>   Seeing you coming.
>
> III. iii. 37–40

Iago is paying out rope, giving just enough for Othello to grab and hold on to. Desdemona pleads Cassio's case and eventually Othello agrees to meet him. Desdemona pledges her love and obedience to Othello before exiting, after which Iago is free to go to work on the Moor. He slyly questions Othello about Cassio's historical relationship with Desdemona, gently but persistently stoking jealousy. Iago feigns backtracking, telling Othello that he is sure all is well and not to worry, even defending Cassio's integrity, but by saying he should observe his wife's interactions with Cassio the damage is done. Othello asks that Emilia and Iago should also be his eyes on Desdemona.

Iago exits and Othello makes a dark soliloquy. As sexual suspicion takes hold, he dangerously starts to formulate and visualize his wrath in advance of any proof:

> If I do prove her haggard,
> Though that her jesses were my dear heart-strings,
> I'ld whistle her off and let her down the wind
> To prey at fortune.

III. iii. 260–263

His language is that of severing affection, drawing on the brutal indifference he has as part of his emotional toolkit. At the same time, the situation starts chipping away at his self-confidence.

Desdemona and Emilia now enter, inviting Othello to dinner. Othello's demeanour is changed. He complains that he has a headache. Desdemona responds by offering to mop his brow with her handkerchief, although she drops it and Othello, significantly, tells her to leave it where it lies. Othello and Desdemona exit, but Emilia remains and finds the handkerchief, explaining its significance and Iago's attraction to it:

> This was her first remembrance from the Moor:
> My wayward husband hath a hundred times
> Woo'd me to steal it; but she so loves the token,
> For he conjured her she should ever keep it

III. iii. 291–294

Despite its import to Desdemona, Emilia says she will copy it and give it to Iago. Then Iago enters. She tells him about the handkerchief and he snatches it greedily. Iago now has a further instrument of deception – he plots to plant the handkerchief in Cassio's lodgings.

Othello enters, wracked in anguish as jealousy's constraining roots wind themselves around his brain and heart. His happiness is purged and all that seemed of value to him previously is now deemed worthless. He angrily confronts Iago to produce evidence, threatening him with grave consequences if there is nothing behind the accusations. Iago defends himself convincingly. Confusion reigns in Othello:

> By the world,
> I think my wife be honest, and think she is not;
> I think that thou art just, and think thou art not:
> I'll have some proof.

III. iii. 383–386

Othello is now governed by passion, trapped in an oscillating logic that takes on an aggressive energy of its own. Iago throws him a bone, saying that he has heard Cassio talk in his dreams about his love for Desdemona and how it must be kept secret. This in itself is enough to meet the burden of proof for Othello, although Iago skilfully argues that it might just be a dream. Then Iago asks Othello about the distinctive handkerchief, saying that he saw Cassio wiping his beard with it. Iago gathers the threads together for Othello:

> If it be that, or any that was hers,
> It speaks against her with the other proofs.
>
> III. iii. 440–441

Note that Iago does not say that he is offering conclusive proof, but rather an overwhelming fusion of circumstantial evidence. It is enough to break Othello's mental logjam, however. He explodes into rage, giving vent to murderous thoughts and a concrete desire for vengeance on both Cassio and Desdemona. Iago pledges his assistance.

Act III, scene iv opens in the company of Emilia, Desdemona and the Clown. Desdemona asks the Clown to find Cassio and, when he has left, frets over the loss of the handkerchief – a symbol of fidelity that is now contaminated to represent fear and distrust. Othello enters and Desdemona makes her firm representation on behalf of Cassio, saying she won't leave until Cassio is reinstated in his post and in Othello's favour. Othello's responses are hot with double meaning. He is hunting for signs – latching on to the moistness of her palm and converting that into evidence of infidelity. He asks to borrow her handkerchief, claiming he has a cold. Desdemona replies that she does not have it. Othello recounts the magical origins and properties of this item, and the disastrous consequences if lost. Desdemona, however, sees the issue of the handkerchief as a distraction from the case of Cassio. Tempers rise and Othello storms out, leaving Emilia reflecting on men's inconstant natures, the swings of their affections.

Iago and Cassio enter. Cassio is downcast and Desdemona explains that, given Othello's current state of mind, now is not the right time for a rapprochement. The talk turns to jealousy. Desdemona is clear that Othello has no reason to be jealous of her; Emilia counters by saying that jealousy doesn't in fact need to be supported by reason. She pinpoints a central dynamic of the play, the detachment of emotion from logic, the two occupying different zones of the psyche, fighting one another for supremacy.

Desdemona and Emilia eventually exit and Bianca – Cassio's mistress – enters. A relatively minor character, Bianca teases out some of the hidden corners of Cassio's character, showing that even the good guys can be less than noble in their relations to women. She complains about Cassio's lack of devotion. Cassio asks her forgiveness, but he also gives her Desdemona's handkerchief and asks her to copy the design so he can return the original item to its owner. She is suspicious of its origins, seeing evidence of another woman. She exits under sufferance.

In **Act IV, scene i**, Iago turns the screws tighter on Othello's burgeoning jealousy. He discusses with Othello the subject of women's propriety – what behaviours are acceptable and what behaviours indicate licentiousness. In reality, he is sawing away at Desdemona's pedestal. Iago ups the ante by taunting Othello with coarse rumours that Cassio has had sex with Desdemona, using barrack-room language to hit home: 'With her, on her; what you will' (IV. i. 34). This accusation, combined with the 'evidence' of the handkerchief, crystallizes Othello's fears to such an extent that he collapses in an epileptic fit. Iago momentarily gloats over his work before Cassio enters, Iago telling him to leave because of Othello's condition.

When Othello comes round, Iago adopts a different strategy for escalation, telling Othello that being cuckolded is a near-universal experience, implying that Desdemona is effectively just like all the rest, knowing this is no consolation. He also explains that Cassio will be returning soon, and instructs Othello to hide and listen to the conversation. Iago confides to the audience that he plans to get Cassio to discuss Bianca, and that Othello will think he refers to Desdemona.

The plan works smoothly. Cassio's discourse on Bianca is ribald and empty, as he explains how he has no intention of marrying her, even though she pursues him lustily and persistently. Off to the side, Othello's anger climbs. Bianca enters but, instead of her presence undoing Iago's scheme, she confronts Cassio over the origins of the handkerchief, seeing it as the gift of another lover. Othello spots the item, and now sees Desdemona as just one in Cassio's promiscuous line-up.

Iago's plan to ensnare 'credulous fools' (IV. i. 46) takes full root and clarifies Othello's purpose: 'How shall I murder him, Iago?' (IV. i. 179). Othello is now whipping himself into a frenzy of violent intent. Iago still guides him by the hand. At one point, Othello declares he will chop Desdemona to bits, then decides to poison her, before Iago steers him towards strangulation. Iago is coaxing out the most bestial side to his nature and giving it purpose.

The two men's machinations are interrupted by the arrival of Lodovico with a letter from the Duke, along with Desdemona. Lodovico, aware of rumours of a split between Cassio and Othello, explains that Othello is to be recalled to Venice, leaving Cassio in command. Desdemona's tender approach to Othello is met with a stinging slap and her dismissal, Othello then exiting. Such behaviour is steadily alienating Othello from both his duty and his reputation. Lodovico ends the scene disillusioned by Othello's character: 'I am sorry that I am deceived in him' (IV. i. 293) – Iago has perfectly engineered Othello's isolation.

In **Act IV, scene ii**, Othello and Emilia are in discussion regarding Desdemona and Cassio. Othello is probing, obsessive. Emilia defends Desdemona, but sense now bounces off Othello, his language becoming ever more vituperative. All Desdemona's potential defences are dismissed in advance, every sign of virtue converted to an indicator of licentious duplicity:

> This is a subtle whore,
> A closet lock and key of villanous secrets:
> And yet she'll kneel and pray

IV. ii. 21–23

Emilia fetches Desdemona. Othello unloads a predatory, distressing interrogation of his wife, who is clearly terrified and confused. She pledges her loyalty, love and fidelity to him, but Othello has her now relabelled a 'whore' and 'strumpet'. Eventually he leaves and the stunned Desdemona asks Emilia to fetch Iago. Shakespeare is once again stacking up the dramatic irony, with Desdemona looking for salvation in the very source of her condemnation. Iago enters and makes sympathetic noises. Emilia, however, correctly suggests that 'some eternal villain' (IV. ii. 130) has poisoned the relationship 'to get some office' (IV. ii. 132). Emilia's voice hints at Iago's potential undoing, since she is a questioning and circumspect witness and not in Iago's thrall. Iago tries to calm her down, quieten her independence of thought.

The two ladies eventually exit and Roderigo joins Iago on stage. He is in a state of agitation, annoyed that Iago seems to have played him for a fool, burning through his money. He threatens to reveal the truth to Desdemona, but again Iago brings him back in line. He explains that Othello intends to take Desdemona to Mauritania. To delay the couple on Cyprus, Roderigo must murder Cassio – Iago promises that later he will give further convincing reasons for this action.

Act IV, scene iii pauses the dramatic pace as Emilia and Desdemona play out a deep discussion of male and female relations, especially in terms of sexual propriety and social inequality. We see two contrasting individuals. Desdemona is crestfallen, vulnerable, poetic and ethereal; Emilia is hardened, realistic, clear-sighted and angry. Thus while Emilia wishes Desdemona had never met Othello, Desdemona dutifully affirms her love for her disaffected husband. Emilia argues that adultery is in fact a 'small vice' (IV. iii. 70) and its condemnation a matter of social convention. In contrast, Desdemona holds to virtue: 'Beshrew me, if I would do such a wrong / For the whole world' (IV. iii. 78–79). She plaintively sings a mournful and death-bound song of heartbreak she heard from a childhood maid called Barbary. Emilia, by contrast, gives a rigorous dissection of gender, saying how male mistreatment of wives often causes their straying in the first place. The scene puts men, and social double standards, under an uncomfortably harsh interrogator.

From **Act V, scene i,** the violence that has been latent in Othello is finally unleashed as he makes his precipitous fall from sanity and grace, unable to contain the furnace-like heat of his anger. The scene opens with Iago giving Roderigo instructions to ambush and kill Cassio. Iago is clearly not Roderigo's ally – when he is alone, he openly states his contempt for Roderigo and that his death will also be necessary. Roderigo follows through and attacks Cassio, but Cassio defends himself, piercing Roderigo with a wounding sword strike. Iago, however, makes a sneak attack from behind and injures Cassio in the leg; Cassio is not aware of the identity of this attacker. The shouts bring Othello, Lodovico and Gratiano to the scene, Iago presenting himself as if he has just been roused from bed. He pretends to search for Cassio's attackers but, on finding the wounded Roderigo, stabs him to death, before returning to tend Cassio's wounds. He feigns trauma when the corpse of Roderigo is discovered.

Emilia and Bianca now enter the stage, shifting the dynamic away from impulsive male violence to sceptical female understanding. Iago turns on Bianca, casting suspicions that she is involved with the attack on Cassio, using stock misogyny to assault her character. He tells Emilia to inform Othello and Desdemona about what has happened. In a final aside, Iago knows that victory or defeat is imminent: 'This is the night / That either makes me or fordoes me quite.' (V. i. 128–129).

Act V, scene ii brings the dire denouement. At its opening, Othello looms like a conflicted beast over sleeping Desdemona. He appeals to celestial bodies to witness the justice of his actions, but also buckles under his confrontation with her face and body, which still captivate him. Desdemona awakes to find her husband transformed with adrenaline – shaking, biting his lip, his eyes rolling. He is beyond control. He gradually unveils his accusations, confronting her about the handkerchief – she replies that Cassio must have found it. Othello urges her to a confession she cannot make, and despite final pleadings for her life, he smothers her.

Emilia is outside. Hearing the noises within, she enquires about their cause, then enters and is confronted with Desdemona's body. Othello makes portentous laments about the killing, but Emilia, true to her character, grounds the scene in tawdry reality: 'O, my good lord, yonder's foul murders done!' (V. ii. 106). The screws start to tighten on Othello when Desdemona momentarily recovers, crying out 'O, falsely, falsely murder'd!' (V. ii. 117). Desdemona's gentleness is reinforced when, in her final words, she claims responsibility for own death, despite attesting she is 'guiltless' (V. ii. 122). She dies.

Emilia turns on Othello, pulling out his confession, which is infused with wandering sexual condemnation of Desdemona. He tells Emilia that it was Iago – the 'honest man' (V. ii. 148) – who convinced him. She cries out murder and Montano, Gratiano, Iago and others enter. Emilia rounds on her husband as liar. Her clarity steadily chips away the artifice both men have erected. Iago's capacity for garrulous deception now squirms under common-sense questioning:

> Iago.   I told him what I thought, and told no more
>   Than what he found himself was apt and true.
> Emil.   But did you ever tell him she was false?
> Iago.   I did.
> Emil.   You told a lie, an odious, damned lie;
>   Upon my soul, a lie, a wicked lie!
>
> V. ii. 176–181

Her language is plain, her accusations sharp. Othello is starting to see the horror of what he has done, truly confirmed when Emilia reveals that she found Desdemona's handkerchief and gave it to Iago.

Iago races to silence Emilia as he faces a dynamic he can't control – his wife has to break the bonds of marital subservience to reveal sin and release justice. Iago defaults to the crudest option for silencing women: violence. He attempts to stab Emilia, then shortly afterwards succeeds in mortally wounding her. He runs out, pursued by Montano and Gratiano.

Emilia dies in Othello's presence, and Othello drowns in his guilt, a slave to self-contempt and grief:

> O cursed slave!
> Whip me, ye devils,
> From the possession of this heavenly sight!
> Blow me about in winds! roast me in sulphur!
> Wash me in steep-down gulfs of liquid fire!
> O Desdemona! Desdemona! dead!
>
> V. ii. 276–281

The other men now return, with Iago as their prisoner. Furious, Othello wounds Iago. Lodovico says that he has confessed. Othello then demands that Iago explain his motives. Crucially, Iago replies that he will not say anything. He is true to his word, not speaking again in the play. This act creates a black hole of possibility in our assessment of his character. Has he run out of deceitful words or is this part of his power play? Does he simply not know why he has done what he has done?

His future, however, is set – Lodovico gives orders that he is to be taken away for imprisonment and torture. Othello, finally destroyed by the clarity of what he has done, stabs himself and dies. There is no sense of final dramatic restoration. The play almost trickles away. Lodovico's words 'The object poisons sight / Let it be hid' (V. ii. 364–365) give sense of a sordid episode to be concealed, and Othello a failure to be forgotten.

ANALYSIS – OTHELLO AND IAGO

Othello might have his name on the poster, but in many ways Iago is the lead character of the play. He occupies far more of the drama's real estate, and is also, in effect, the conductor of much of its action. He is like a stake driven into the ground in the centre of the play, all other characters tied to him with varying lengths of rope.

That Iago is a villain, there is no doubt. He is ruthless and destructive, manipulative and cruel, astoundingly amoral. He treats people like unwanted toys to be broken in rough play. He bears inner hostility towards most of the play's characters, cruelly deceiving them in the process and guiding many towards death, even at his own hand. The extent of his villainy is appalling, but one key question remains open: why?

We find only slim motives for the magnitude of his malevolence. He is jealous of Cassio's promotion and angry at Othello for overlooking him. He suggests that Othello has slept with his wife Emilia, possibly Cassio too. But none of these hold much factual weight, nor appear with frequency enough to suggest they are abidingly believed. The evidence of adultery is scant, and seems more connected with his general misogyny. His contempt for Othello is set against the high regard Othello has for him, and the elevated protestations of loyal service Iago makes openly:

> Iago.   My lord, you know I love you.
> Oth.   I think thou dost;
> And for I know thou'rt full of love and honesty
> And weigh'st thy words before thou givest them breath,
> Therefore these stops of thine fright me the more:

> For such things in a false disloyal knave
> Are tricks of custom; but in a man that's just
> They're close delations, working from the heart,
> That passion cannot rule

III. iii. 117–124

For Othello, Iago is a lighthouse of reassurance. But by this stage, the audience is uncomfortably aware of what 'weigh'st thy words' means for Iago. He is a master of verbal duplicity, skilfully slipping between characters and positions, playing his many parts perfectly.

A perceived lack of concrete motivations in Iago led the Romantic poet and critic Samuel Taylor Coleridge to label him as a 'motiveless malignity'. Certainly, he is a hard character to pin down. We might point to a motive of racism, of which Iago has plenty. He makes frequent grubby references to Othello's blackness – 'an old black ram' (I. i. 88), a devil (I. i. 91), 'a Barbary horse' (I. i. 112). He is also certainly misogynistic. But ultimately, Iago seems something of a vacuum, a human-shaped gap where morality should be. He is a classic sociopath, taking pleasure in the energy of cruel, complicated plots free from the constraints of empathy. In many ways the scheming is the purpose itself: 'Dull not device by coldness and delay' (II. iii. 394), says Iago. Don't think, act.

We can link Coleridge's claim to two quotations from opposite ends of the play. In the very first scene, Iago tells Roderigo 'I am not what I am' (I. i. 65). While Iago here openly confesses the mismatch between his outer, public persona and his internal motivations, he does not dig deep with explanation. At the very end of the play, as we have seen, his final words are a further embrace of opacity:

> Demand me nothing; what you know, you know:
> From this time forth I never will speak word.

V. ii. 303–304

The key element of this passage is 'what you know, you know'. It is as if Iago is saying that there is nothing to work out – his actions *are* his character. He makes *us* go to the effort of explaining *him*. Like Othello, Iago is making us fill in the blanks. This is Iago's critical device. If he demonstrates anything, it is that his skill is getting others to complete his villainy. Often he simply gives them direction and suspicion, and they do all the rest. In Act II, scene iii, he reaches out to the audience, challenging them to define the extent of his guilt:

> And what's he then that says I play the villain?
> When this advice is free I give and honest

II. ii. 342–343

In effect he is saying 'I'm not to blame'. He feeds others a little kindling, and they fan the flames all themselves.

We see this effect in several secondary characters. Roderigo is a weak individual easily moved by Iago's words, a pawn whom Iago regards with contempt as 'poor trash of Venice' (II. i. 312). Cassio is driven through fear of loss of reputation, leaving him exposed to manipulation. Indeed, Iago sees that Cassio has the requisite qualities to be dominated by strong characters:

> the knave is handsome, young, and hath
> all those requisites in him that folly and green
> minds look after

II. i. 250–252

From these lines, we can perhaps detect in Iago a simple desire to crush virtue and happiness, inexplicable but not implausible.

The most significant of Iago's victims is, of course, Othello. For Shakespeare's audiences, Othello's race would be at least a consideration in his downfall. Othello was not the first Moor in Jacobean drama – that honour goes to the character Muly Mahamet in George Peele's *The Battle of Alcazar* (c. 1591). In that play, Muly is underhand and duplicitous, but the Moorish king Abdelmelec has higher values. Crucially, Abdelmelec is rendered as fairer in skin tone while Muly's skin is deep black – Renaissance audiences generally made clear connections between outward appearance and inner character.

Initially, Othello is presented as a figure of nobility and bearing, a straight-speaking soldier and proven leader of men, now softened somewhat by love. He wins us over with a tender and warmly logical defence of his relationship with Desdemona:

> She loved me for the dangers I had pass'd,
> And I loved her that she did pity them.
> This only is the witchcraft I have used

I. iii. 167–169

But at the same time, we are made aware that Othello's profession means he is a man who can override sentiment in favour of brutal action. Here he tamps down the concerns of the senators that his new-found love will distract him from his martial duties:

The tyrant custom, most grave senators,
Hath made the flinty and steel couch of war
My thrice-driven bed of down: I do agnize
A natural and prompt alacrity
I find in hardness

I. iii. 230–234

We sense the man capable of violence. The degree to which this is specifically connected to his race is debatable. Certainly, Othello is subject to racial slurs – base examples include 'thick lips' (I. i. 66) and 'sooty bosom' (I. ii. 70). Othello himself appears at times self-conscious of his race and its social implications, such as when he says of Desdemona that 'she had eyes, and chose me' (III. iii. 189). There is the suggestion here that his ethnicity is something to get past, or at least to negotiate, for outsiders. The Duke says to Brabantio: 'Your son-in-law is far more fair than black' (I. iii. 291) – this compliment is backhanded, suggesting that Othello has somehow escaped blackness.

Tragically, however, any 'fairness' in Othello's character is smothered by rising, swirling jealously, which brings out horrifying cruelty and laser-like unreason. Critics have been divided over the degree of Othello's culpability for the destruction of Desdemona – how much was he led to his actions, and how much did he lead himself? Iago knows, however, that, once ignited, jealousy will do much of its own work, without considered evidence:

I speak not yet of proof.
Look to your wife: observe her well with Cassio;
Wear your eye thus, not jealous nor secure

III. iii. 196–198

Iago winds Othello in through allusion and suggestion, not facts. Here it may be that Shakespeare was influenced by John Leo's *A Geographical Historie of Africa*, published in translation in 1600. Leo was himself a Moor, and provided a psychological picture of his people, saying that they were proud, dignified and noble, but that 'no nation in the world is so subject unto jealousy; for they will rather lose their lives than put up any disgrace in the behalf of their women.'

Once Othello gives in to jealousy, it possesses him completely. Emilia explains the self-feeding mechanism at work:

Des.   Alas the day, I never gave him cause!
Emil.   But jealous souls will not be answer'd so;

> They are not ever jealous for the cause,
> But jealous for they are jealous: 'tis a monster
> Begot upon itself, born on itself.
>
> III. iv. 158–162

Emilia presents jealousy exponentially propagating itself. Once it takes hold, Othello's language becomes contaminated. The imagery of poisoning appears frequently, as if jealousy is a slow-acting agent seeping through Othello's bloodstream, as Iago observes:

> The Moor already changes with my poison:
> Dangerous conceits are in their natures poisons,
> Which at the first are scarce found to distaste,
> But with a little act upon the blood
> Burn like the mines of sulphur
>
> III. iii. 325–329

Taking the overview, can we say that Othello's downfall begins with Iago's poison, but in Shakespeare's presentation is it Othello's 'blood' – his race – upon which the poison acts? Was Shakespeare conforming to race stereotypes? Some of the other characters reach for this conclusion. After the murder of Desdemona, for example, Emilia calls Othello a 'filthy bargain' (V. ii. 157). Othello also appears to meet racial self-loathing, likening himself to a 'base Indian' (V. ii. 347) and a 'malignant and a turban'd Turk' (V. ii. 353).

Increasingly, *Othello* is seen as a problematic play in relation to its portrayal of race. But while Shakespeare certainly plugs into contemporary attitudes to race, he complicates the picture. Notably, the most corrupting figure is white – Othello's sins are anger and jealousy, crude emotional responses, but Iago's sins are legion and finely crafted, Machiavellian in the Renaissance understanding of the term. Othello has a noble character corrupted, and he is ultimately cognizant of his own dreadful failings. His downfall is tragic, not welcomed by us (as in the case of Iago), and there remains something of his greatness even at the end of the play.

THE WOMEN OF *OTHELLO*

If Othello makes a partial challenge to racism, it could be argued that Desdemona and Emilia make their own imperfect, hobbled assault on misogyny and gender conventions. In many ways, Desdemona is pure victim. Once Othello's jealousy takes root, she is effectively condemned, trapped by crude sexual stereotypes and Othello's own pathology. By the final scenes, she is little more than a frightened, vulnerable young woman, unable to escape his power or assuage his suspicion. Yet this subjugation by physical power should not mask Desdemona's spirit of independence, challenging to Renaissance mores. By marrying Othello, a Moor, secretly and without her father's blessing, she undermines convention on multiple levels, giving personal agency an authority over what society deems fitting. In the defence of her marriage to Othello, it is clear that Desdemona knows her own mind, and understands that if she is to subvert propriety then she must be able to explain why:

> My noble father,
> I do perceive here a divided duty:
> To you I am bound for life and education;
> My life and education both do learn me
> How to respect you; you are the lord of duty,
> I am hitherto your daughter: but here's my
> husband

I. iii. 180–185

Here Desdemona is presenting a romantic, emotional impulse also as a logical act, giving emotions a greater weight in the balance scales of argument. This resistance comes unexpected to Brabantio, who says:

> A maiden never bold;
> Of spirit so still and quiet that her motion
> Blush'd at herself; and she—in spite of nature,
> Of years, of country, credit, every thing—
> To fall in love with what she fear'd to look on!

I. iii. 94–98

Again, Brabantio brings race to the fore, curling his lip at the way Desdemona has fallen in love with what he sees as a pairing that required her to recalibrate her decency. The impression of Brabantio is a man alienated from his daughter – he doesn't truly know her, and cannot see the woman she has become.

Part of Desdemona's independence, and an unfortunate ingredient in her destruction, is also her sexuality. She is presented as sensual, her passions directed squarely to Othello, physically cementing their love. Only later does Othello turn her sexuality into something sordid, defining her horribly as 'that cunning whore of Venice' (IV. ii. 89). Desdemona stays faithful to, if frightened of, Othello, as progressively her husband strips her of her worth and agency, leading to her death. Her murder is a severe judgement upon Othello and Iago, but perhaps also the male characters' general gaze, which both encourages and condemns female sexuality.

Emilia has a very different evolution to Desdemona, as she climbs up through male power to become one of the most commanding moral voices in the play. The audience has to negotiate the fact that she is, ultimately, Iago's wife, a fact that brings some measure of implicit guilt. Doesn't she know what he is like? She also participates in stealing Desdemona's handkerchief, an action that has grave consequences and shows a strange thrall to her obviously deviant husband.

So Emilia is no paragon of virtue. But eventually this positioning works to her strength. She is something of an insider, more aware of men's tricks and desires. She also becomes a victim of male violence, when Iago kills her. But before then, and more than Desdemona, she finds the voice to confront the injustices of contemporary gender politics. Her words scrutinize male appetites with the weary rigour of experience:

> 'Tis not a year or two shows us a man:
> They are all but stomachs and we all but food;
> They eat us hungerly, and when they are full
> They belch us.
>
> III. iv. 103–106

Here is the voice of the realist. Emilia throws out a challenge to the audience, asking them to reflect on what it means to be a woman in a male-dominated society. By the end of the play, Emilia's voice finds its full, explosive and public expression, rounding on her husband following Desdemona's murder:

> *Iago.* 'Zounds! hold your peace.
> *Emil.*   'Twill out, 'twill out. I peace!
> No, I will speak as liberal as the north:
> Let heaven and men and devils, let them all,
> All, all, cry shame against me, yet I'll speak.
>
> V. ii. 219–222

Unfortunately, she pays the price for her resistance, but her accusations are vital to unmask and debunk Iago. At some level, Iago is an engaging dramatic figure – he offers a relentless energy and guile, superb wordplay, intelligent manipulation. It is easy for the audience to get caught up in his pulsing energy. Emilia, however, exposes the hollowness, the malign vacuity, behind this front, and reminds us of the real-world effects upon the vulnerable. She turns informer, inquisitor, when the injustice reaches intolerable levels.

As with many of Shakespeare's great tragedies, *Othello* is a haunting work, leaving unresolved questions in the audience's mind long after they have left the theatre. The drama compels us to make at least some attempt to understand the nature of evil, and the part that good people can play in evil's manifestations. Crucially, it confronts society with moral questions about the complex relationships between power, virtue and psychology, and hence achieves that timelessness for which Shakespeare is renowned.

THE TRAGEDY OF OTHELLO, THE MOOR OF VENICE

DRAMATIS PERSONÆ

DUKE OF VENICE.
BRABANTIO, *a senator.*
Other Senators.
GRATIANO, *brother to Brabantio.*
LODOVICO, *kinsman to Brabantio.*
OTHELLO, *a noble Moor in the service of the Venetian state.*
CASSIO, *his lieutenant.*
IAGO, *his ancient.*
RODERIGO, *a Venetian gentleman.*
MONTANO, *Othello's predecessor in the government of Cyprus.*
CLOWN, *servant to Othello.*

DESDEMONA, *daughter to Brabantio and wife to Othello.*
EMILIA, *wife to Iago.*
BIANCA, *mistress to Cassio.*

Sailor, Messenger, Herald, Officers, Gentlemen,
Musicians, and Attendants..

SCENE: *Venice: a seaport in Cyprus.*

OTHELLO, THE MOOR OF VENICE

ACT FIRST
SCENE I

Venice. A street .

Enter Roderigo and Iago.

Rod. Tush, never tell me; I take it much unkindly
That thou, Iago, who hast had my purse
As if the strings were thine, shouldst know of this.

Iago. 'Sblood, but you will not hear me:
If ever I did dream of such a matter,
Abhor me.

Rod. Thou told'st me thou didst hold him in thy hate.

Iago. Despise me, if I do not. Three great ones of
        the city,
In personal suit to make me his lieutenant,
Off-capp'd to him: and, by the faith of man,   10
I know my price, I am worth no worse a place.
But he, as loving his own pride and purposes,
Evades them, with a bombast circumstance
Horribly stuff'd with epithets of war;
And, in conclusion,
Nonsuits my mediators; for, 'Certes,' says he,
'I have already chose my officer.'
And what was he?
Forsooth, a great arithmetician,
One Michael Cassio, a Florentine,   20
A fellow almost damn'd in a fair wife;
That never set a squadron in the field,
Nor the division of a battle knows
More than a spinster; unless the bookish theoric,

Wherein the toged consuls can propose
As masterly as he: mere prattle without practice
Is all his soldiership. But he, sir, had the election:
And I, of whom his eyes had seen the proof
At Rhodes, at Cyprus, and on other grounds
Christian and heathen, must be be-lee'd and calm'd   30
By debitor and creditor: this counter-caster,
He, in good time, must his lieutenant be,
And I—God bless the mark!—his Moorship's
           ancient.

Rod.   By heaven, I rather would have been his
           hangman.

Iago.   Why, there's no remedy; 'tis the curse of service,
Preferment goes by letter and affection,
And not by old gradation, where each second
Stood heir to the first. Now, sir, be judge yourself
Whether I in any just term am affined
To love the Moor.

Rod.   I would not follow him then.   40

Iago.   O, sir, content you;
I follow him to serve my turn upon him:
We cannot all be masters, nor all masters
Cannot be truly follow'd. You shall mark
Many a duteous and knee-crooking knave,
That doting on his own obsequious bondage
Wears out his time, much like his master's ass,
For nought but provender, and when he's old,
           cashier'd:
Whip me such honest knaves. Others there are
Who, trimm'd in forms and visages of duty,   50
Keep yet their hearts attending on themselves,
And throwing but shows of service on their lords
Do well thrive by them, and when they have
           lined their coats
Do themselves homage: these fellows have some
           soul,
And such a one do I profess myself.
For, sir.

It is as sure as you are Roderigo,
Were I the Moor, I would not be Iago:
In following him, I follow but myself;
Heaven is my judge, not I for love and duty,
But seeming so, for my peculiar end: 60
For when my outward action doth demonstrate
The native act and figure of my heart
In compliment extern, 'tis not long after
But I will wear my heart upon my sleeve
For daws to peck at: I am not what I am.

Rod.   What a full fortune does the thick lips owe,
If he can carry 't thus!

Iago.   Call up her father,
Rouse him: make after him, poison his delight,
Proclaim him in the streets; incense her kinsmen,
And, though he in a fertile climate dwell,   70
Plague him with flies: though that his joy be joy,
Yet throw such changes of vexation on 't
As it may lose some colour.

Rod.   Here is her father's house; I'll call aloud.

Iago.   Do; with like timorous accent and dire yell
As when, by night and negligence, the fire
Is spied in populous cities.

Rod.   What, ho, Brabantio! Signior Brabantio, ho!

Iago.   Awake! what, ho, Brabantio! thieves! thieves!
             thieves!
Look to your house, your daughter and your bags!   80
Thieves! thieves!

Brabantio appears above, at a window.

Bra.   What is the reason of this terrible summons?
What is the matter there?

Rod.   Signior, is all your family within?

Iago.   Are your doors lock'd?

Bra.   Why, wherefore ask you this?

Iago.   'Zounds, sir, you're robb'd; for shame, put on
                 your gown;
     Your heart is burst, you have lost half your soul;
     Even now, now, very now, an old black ram
     Is tupping your white ewe. Arise, arise;
     Awake the snorting citizens with the bell,   90
     Or else the devil will make a grandsire of you:
     Arise, I say.

Bra.   What, have you lost your wits?

Rod.   Most reverend signior, do you know my voice?

Bra.   Not I: what are you?

Rod.   My name is Roderigo.

Bra.   The worser welcome:
     I have charged thee not to haunt about my doors;
     In honest plainness thou hast heard me say
     My daughter is not for thee; and now, in madness,
     Being full of supper and distempering draughts,
     Upon malicious bravery, dost thou come   100
     To start my quiet.

Rod.   Sir, sir, sir,—

Bra.   But thou must needs be sure
     My spirit and my place have in them power
     To make this bitter to thee.

Rod.   Patience, good sir.

Bra.   What tell'st thou me of robbing? this is Venice;
     My house is not a grange.

Rod.   Most grave Brabantio,
     In simple and pure soul I come to you.

Iago.   'Zounds, sir, you are one of those that will not
     serve God, if the devil bid you. Because we
     come to do you service and you think we are
     ruffians, you'll have your daughter covered   110
     with a Barbary horse; you'll have your nephews
     neigh to you; you'll have coursers for cousins,

and gennets for germans.

Bra. What profane wretch art thou?

Iago. I am one, sir, that comes to tell you your
daughter and the Moor are now making the
beast with two backs.

Bra. Thou art a villain.

Iago.   You are—a senator.

Bra. This thou shalt answer; I know thee, Roderigo.   120

Rod. Sir, I will answer any thing. But, I beseech you,
If 't be your pleasure and most wise consent,
As partly I find it is, that your fair daughter,
At this odd-even and dull watch o' the night,
Transported with no worse nor better guard
But with a knave of common hire, a gondolier,
To the gross clasps of a lascivious Moor,—
If this be known to you, and your allowance,
We then have done you bold and saucy wrongs;
But if you know not this, my manners tell me   130
We have your wrong rebuke. Do not believe
That, from the sense of all civility,
I thus would play and trifle with your reverence:
Your daughter, if you have not given her leave,
I say again, hath made a gross revolt,
Tying her duty, beauty, wit and fortunes,
In an extravagant and wheeling stranger
Of here and every where. Straight satisfy yourself:
If she be in her chamber or your house,
Let loose on me the justice of the state   140
For thus deluding you.

Bra.   Strike on the tinder, ho!
Give me a taper! call up all my people!
This accident is not unlike my dream:
Belief of it oppresses me already.
Light, I say! light!   [*Exit above.*

Iago.   Farewell; for I must leave you:
It seems not meet, nor wholesome to my place,

To be produced—as, if I stay, I shall—
Against the Moor: for I do know, the state,
However this may gall him with some check,
Cannot with safety cast him; for he's embark'd   150
With such loud reason to the Cyprus wars,
Which even now stand in act, that, for their souls,
Another of his fathom they have none
To lead their business: in which regard,
Though I do hate him as I do hell pains,
Yet for necessity of present life,
I must show out a flag and sign of love,
Which is indeed but sign. That you shall surely
    find him,
Lead to the Sagittary the raised search;
And there will I be with him. So farewell.   [*Exit.*   160

*Enter, below, Brabantio, in his night-gown, and Servants
with torches.*

Bra.   It is too true an evil: gone she is;
And what's to come of my despised time
Is nought but bitterness. Now, Roderigo,
Where didst thou see her? O unhappy girl!
With the Moor, say'st thou? Who would be
    a father!
How didst thou know 'twas she? O, she
    deceives me
Past thought! What said she to you? Get more
    tapers.
Raise all my kindred. Are they married, think you?

Rod.   Truly, I think they are.

Bra.   O heaven! How got she out? O treason of the
    blood!   170
Fathers, from hence trust not your daughters' minds
By what you see them act. Is there not charms
By which the property of youth and maidhood
May be abused? Have you not read, Roderigo,
Of some such thing?

Rod.   Yes, sir, I have indeed.

Bra. Call up my brother. O, would you had had her!
Some one way, some another. Do you know
Where we may apprehend her and the Moor?

Rod. I think I can discover him, if you please
To get good guard and go along with me.   180

Bra. Pray you, lead on. At every house I'll call;
I may command at most. Get weapons, ho!
And raise some special officers of night.
On, good Roderigo; I'll deserve your pains.   [*Exeunt.*

SCENE II

———➩●◄———

Another street.

Enter Othello, Iago, and Attendants with torches..

Iago. Though in the trade of war I have slain men,
Yet do I hold it very stuff o' the conscience
To do no contrived murder: I lack iniquity
Sometimes to do me service: nine or ten times
I had thought to have yerk'd him here under
                the ribs.

Oth. 'Tis better as it is.

Iago.   Nay, but he prated
And spoke such scurvy and provoking terms
Against your honour,
That, with the little godliness I have,
I did full hard forbear him. But I pray you, sir,   10
Are you fast married? Be assured of this,
That the magnifico is much beloved,
And hath in his effect a voice potential
As double as the duke's: he will divorce you,
Or put upon you what restraint and grievance
The law, with all his might to enforce it on,
Will give him cable.

Oth.   Let him do his spite:
My services, which I have done the signiory,
Shall out-tongue his complaints. 'Tis yet to
            know—
Which, when I know that boasting is an honour,   20
I shall promulgate—I fetch my life and being
From men of royal siege, and my demerits
May speak unbonneted to as proud a fortune
As this that I have reach'd: for know, Iago,
But that I love the gentle Desdemona,
I would not my unhoused free condition
Put into circumscription and confine
For the sea's worth. But, look! what lights come
            yond?

Iago. Those are the raised father and his friends:
You were best go in.

Oth.   Not I; I must be found: 30
My parts, my title and my perfect soul,
Shall manifest me rightly. Is it they?

Iago. By Janus, I think no.

Enter Cassio, and certain Officers with torches.

Oth. The servants of the duke, and my lieutenant.
The goodness of the night upon you, friends!
What is the news?

Cas.   The duke does greet you, general,
And he requires your haste-post-haste appearance,
Even on the instant.

Oth.   What is the matter, think you?

Cas. Something from Cyprus, as I may divine:
It is a business of some heat: the galleys   40
Have sent a dozen sequent messengers
This very night at one another's heels;
And many of the consuls, raised and met,
Are at the duke's already: you have been hotly
            call'd for;
When, being not at your lodging to be found,

       The senate hath sent about three several quests
       To search you out.

Oth.   'Tis well I am found by you.
       I will but spend a word here in the house,
       And go with you.   [*Exit.*

Cas.   Ancient, what makes he here?

Iago. Faith, he to-night hath boarded a land carack: 50
       If it prove lawful prize, he's made for ever.

Cas. I do not understand.

Iago.   He's married.

Cas.   To who?

Re-enter Othello.

Iago. Marry, to—Come, captain, will you go?

Oth.   Have with you.

Cas. Here comes another troop to seek for you.

Iago. It is Brabantio: general, be advised;
       He comes to bad intent.

*Enter Brabantio, Roderigo, and Officers with torches
and weapons.*

Oth.   Holla! stand there!

Rod. Signior, it is the Moor.

Bra.   Down with him, thief!
        [*They draw on both sides.*

Iago. You, Roderigo! come, sir, I am for you.

Oth. Keep up your bright swords, for the dew will
       rust them.
       Good signior, you shall more command with years 60
       Than with your weapons.

Bra. O thou foul thief, where hast thou stow'd my
       daughter?

Damn'd as thou art, thou hast enchanted her;
For I'll refer me to all things of sense,
If she in chains of magic were not bound,
Whether a maid so tender, fair and happy,
So opposite to marriage that she shunn'd
The wealthy curled darlings of our nation,
Would ever have, to incur a general mock,
Run from her guardage to the sooty bosom   70
Of such a thing as thou, to fear, not to delight.
Judge me the world, if 'tis not gross in sense
That thou hast practised on her with foul charms,
Abused her delicate youth with drugs or minerals
That weaken motion: I'll have 't disputed on;
'Tis probable, and palpable to thinking.
I therefore apprehend and do attach thee
For an abuser of the world, a practiser
Of arts inhibited and out of warrant.
Lay hold upon him: if he do resist,   80
Subdue him at his peril.

Oth.   Hold your hands,
Both you of my inclining and the rest:
Were it my cue to fight, I should have known it
Without a prompter. Where will you that I go
To answer this your charge?

Bra.   To prison, till fit time
Of law and course of direct session
Call thee to answer.

Oth.   What if I do obey?
How may the duke be therewith satisfied,
Whose messengers are here about my side,
Upon some present business of the state   90
To bring me to him?

First Off.   'Tis true, most worthy signior;
The duke's in council, and your noble self,
I am sure, is sent for.

Bra.   How! the duke in council!
In this time of the night! Bring him away:

42

Mine's not an idle cause: the duke himself,
Or any of my brothers of the state,
Cannot but feel this wrong as 'twere their own;
For if such actions may have passage free,
Bond-slaves and pagans shall our statesmen be.   [*Exeunt.*

SCENE III

A council-chamber.

The Duke and Senators sitting at a table; Officers attending.

Duke. There is no composition in these news
      That gives them credit.

First Sen.   Indeed they are disproportion'd;
      My letters say a hundred and seven galleys.

Duke. And mine, a hundred and forty.

Sec. Sen.   And mine, two hundred:
      But though they jump not on a just account,—
      As in these cases, where the aim reports,
      'Tis oft with difference,—yet do they all confirm
      A Turkish fleet, and bearing up to Cyprus.

Duke. Nay, it is possible enough to judgement:
      I do not so secure me in the error,   10
      But the main article I do approve
      In fearful sense.

Sailor.   [*Within*] What, ho! what, ho! what, ho!

First Off. A messenger from the galleys.

Enter Sailor.

Duke.   Now, what's the business?

Sail.   The Turkish preparation makes for Rhodes;

43

So was I bid report here to the state
By Signior Angelo.

Duke. How say you by this change?

First Sen.   This cannot be,
        By no assay of reason: 'tis a pageant
        To keep us in false gaze. When we consider
        The importancy of Cyprus to the Turk,   20
        And let ourselves again but understand
        That as it more concerns the Turk than Rhodes,
        So may he with more facile question bear it,
        For that it stands not in such warlike brace,
        But altogether lacks the abilities
        That Rhodes is dress'd in: if we make thought
                    of this,
        We must not think the Turk is so unskilful
        To leave that latest which concerns him first,
        Neglecting an attempt of ease and gain,
        To wake and wage a danger profitless.   30

Duke. Nay, in all confidence, he's not for Rhodes.

First Off. Here is more news.

Enter a Messenger.

Mess. The Ottomites, reverend and gracious,
        Steering with due course toward the isle of Rhodes,
        Have there injointed them with an after fleet.

First Sen. Ay, so I thought. How many, as you guess?

Mess. Of thirty sail: and now they do re-stem
        Their backward course, bearing with frank appearance
        Their purposes toward Cyprus. Signior Montano,
        Your trusty and most valiant servitor,   40
        With his free duty recommends you thus,
        And prays you to believe him.

Duke. 'Tis certain then for Cyprus.
        Marcus Luccicos, is not he in town?

First Sen. He's now in Florence.

Duke. Write from us to him; post-post-haste dispatch.

First Sen. Here comes Brabantio and the valiant Moor.

Enter Brabantio, Othello, Iago, Roderigo, and Officers.

Duke.   Valiant Othello, we must straight employ you
        Against the general enemy Ottoman.
        [*To Brabantio*] I did not see you; welcome,
                    gentle signior;   50
        We lack'd your counsel and your help to-night.

Bra.   So did I yours. Good your grace, pardon me;
        Neither my place nor aught I heard of business
        Hath raised me from my bed, nor doth the
                  general care
        Take hold on me; for my particular grief
        Is of so flood-gate and o'erbearing nature
        That it engluts and swallows other sorrows,
        And it is still itself.

Duke.   Why, what's the matter?

Bra.   My daughter! O, my daughter!

All.   Dead?

Bra.   Ay, to me;
        She is abused, stol'n from me and corrupted   60
        By spells and medicines bought of mountebanks;
        For nature so preposterously to err,
        Being not deficient, blind, or lame of sense,
        Sans witchcraft could not.

Duke.   Whoe'er he be that in this foul proceeding
        Hath thus beguiled your daughter of herself
        And you of her, the bloody book of law
        You shall yourself read in the bitter letter
        After your own sense, yea, though our
                proper son
        Stood in your action.

Bra.   Humbly I thank your grace.   70
        Here is the man, this Moor; whom now, it seems,
        Your special mandate for the state-affairs
        Hath hither brought.

All.   We are very sorry for 't.

Duke. [*To Othello*] What in your own part can you
             say to this?

Bra. Nothing, but this is so.

Oth. Most potent, grave, and reverend signiors,
My very noble and approved good masters,
That I have ta'en away this old man's daughter,
It is most true; true, I have married her:
The very head and front of my offending   80
Hath this extent, no more. Rude am I in my
        speech,
And little blest with the soft phrase of peace;
For since these arms of mine had seven years'
        pith,
Till now some nine moons wasted, they have used
Their dearest action in the tented field;
And little of this great world can I speak,
More than pertains to feats of broil and battle;
And therefore little shall I grace my cause
In speaking for myself. Yet, by your gracious
        patience,
I will a round unvarnish'd tale deliver   90
Of my whole course of love; what drugs, what
        charms,
What conjuration and what mighty magic—
For such proceeding I am charged withal—
I won his daughter.

Bra.   A maiden never bold;
Of spirit so still and quiet that her motion
Blush'd at herself; and she—in spite of nature,
Of years, of country, credit, every thing—
To fall in love with what she fear'd to look on!
It is a judgement maim'd and most imperfect,
That will confess perfection so could err   100
Against all rules of nature; and must be driven
To find out practices of cunning hell,
Why this should be. I therefore vouch again,
That with some mixtures powerful o'er the blood,

46

Or with some dram conjured to this effect,
He wrought upon her.

Duke.   To vouch this, is no proof,
Without more certain and more overt test
Than these thin habits and poor likelihoods
Of modern seeming do prefer against him.

First Sen. But, Othello, speak: 110
Did you by indirect and forced courses
Subdue and poison this young maid's affections?
Or came it by request, and such fair question
As soul to soul affordeth?

Oth.   I do beseech you,
Send for the lady to the Sagittary,
And let her speak of me before her father:
If you do find me foul in her report,
The trust, the office I do hold of you,
Not only take away, but let your sentence
Even fall upon my life.

Duke.   Fetch Desdemona hither, 120

Oth. Ancient, conduct them; you best know the place.
                    [*Exeunt Iago and Attendants.*
And till she come, as truly as to heaven
I do confess the vices of my blood,
So justly to your grave ears I'll present
How I did thrive in this fair lady's love
And she in mine.

Duke. Say it, Othello.

Oth. Her father loved me, oft invited me,
Still questioned me the story of my life
From year to year, the battles, sieges, fortunes, 130
That I have pass'd.
I ran it through, even from my boyish days
To the very moment that he bade me tell it:
Wherein I spake of most disastrous chances,
Of moving accidents by flood and field,
Of hair-breadth 'scapes i' the imminent deadly
                    breach,

Of being taken by the insolent foe,
And sold to slavery, of my redemption thence,
And portance in my travels' history:
Wherein of antres vast and deserts idle,
      touch heaven,   140
Rough quarries, rocks, and hills whose heads
It was my hint to speak,—such was the process;
And of the Cannibals that each other eat,
The Anthropophagi, and men whose heads
Do grow beneath their shoulders. This to hear
Would Desdemona seriously incline:
But still the house-affairs would draw her thence;
Which ever as she could with haste dispatch,
She'ld come again, and with a greedy ear
Devour up my discourse: which I observing,   150
Took once a pliant hour, and found good means
To draw from her a prayer of earnest heart
That I would all my pilgrimage dilate,
Whereof by parcels she had something heard,
But not intentively: I did consent,
And often did beguile her of her tears
When I did speak of some distressful stroke
That my youth suffer'd. My story being done,
She gave me for my pains a world of sighs:
She swore, in faith, 'twas strange, 'twas passing strange;   160
'Twas pitiful, 'twas wondrous pitiful:
She wish'd she had not heard it, yet she wish'd
That heaven had made her such a man: she thank'd me,
And bade me, if I had a friend that loved her,
I should but teach him how to tell my story,
And that would woo her. Upon this hint I spake:
She loved me for the dangers I had pass'd,
And I loved her that she did pity them.
This only is the witchcraft I have used.
Here comes the lady; let her witness it.   170

Enter Desdemona, Iago, and Attendants.

  Duke. I think this tale would win my daughter too.
    Good Brabantio,
    Take up this mangled matter at the best:

Men do their broken weapons rather use
Than their bare hands.

Bra.   I pray you, hear her speak:
If she confess that she was half the wooer,
Destruction on my head, if my bad blame
Light on the man! Come hither, gentle mistress:
Do you perceive in all this noble company
Where most you owe obedience?

Des.   My noble father,   180
I do perceive here a divided duty:
To you I am bound for life and education;
My life and education both do learn me
How to respect you; you are the lord of duty,
I am hitherto your daughter: but here's my
                    husband,
And so much duty as my mother show'd
To you, preferring you before her father,
So much I challenge that I may profess
Due to the Moor my lord.

Bra.   God be with you! I have done.
Please it your grace, on to the state-affairs: 190
I had rather to adopt a child than get it.
Come hither, Moor:
I here do give thee that with all my heart,
Which, but thou hast already, with all my heart
I would keep from thee. For your sake, jewel,
I am glad at soul I have no other child;
For thy escape would teach me tyranny,
To hang clogs on them. I have done, my lord.

Duke. Let me speak like yourself, and lay a sentence
Which, as a grise or step, may help these lovers   200
Into your favour.
When remedies are past, the griefs are ended
By seeing the worst, which late on hopes depended.
To mourn a mischief that is past and gone
Is the next way to draw new mischief on.
What cannot be preserved when fortune takes,
Patience her injury a mockery makes.

The robb'd that smiles steals something from
        the thief;
He robs himself that spends a bootless grief.

Bra. So let the Turk of Cyprus us beguile;   210
We lose it not so long as we can smile.
He bears the sentence well, that nothing bears
But the free comfort which from thence he hears;
But he bears both the sentence and the sorrow,
That, to pay grief, must of poor patience borrow.
These sentences, to sugar or to gall,
Being strong on both sides, are equivocal:
But words are words; I never yet did hear
That the bruised heart was pierced through the ear.
I humbly beseech you, proceed to the affairs of
        state.   220

Duke. The Turk with a most mighty preparation
makes for Cyprus. Othello, the fortitude of the
place is best known to you; and though we
have there a substitute of most allowed
sufficiency, yet opinion, a sovereign mistress of
effects, throws a more safer voice on you: you
must therefore be content to slubber the gloss
of your new fortunes with this more stubborn
and boisterous expedition.

Oth. The tyrant custom, most grave senators,   230
Hath made the flinty and steel couch of war
My thrice-driven bed of down: I do agnize
A natural and prompt alacrity
I find in hardness; and do undertake
These present wars against the Ottomites.
Most humbly therefore bending to your state,
I crave fit disposition for my wife,
Due reference of place and exhibition,
With such accommodation and besort
As levels with her breeding.

Duke.   If you please,   240
Be 't at her father's.

Bra.   I'll not have it so.

Oth.   Nor I.

Des.   Nor I, I would not there reside,
        To put my father in impatient thoughts
        By being in his eye. Most gracious duke,
        To my unfolding lend your prosperous ear,
        And let me find a charter in your voice
        To assist my simpleness.

Duke. What would you, Desdemona?

Des.   That I did love the Moor to live with him,
         My downright violence and storm of fortunes   250
         May trumpet to the world: my heart's subdued
         Even to the very quality of my lord:
         I saw Othello's visage in his mind,
         And to his honours and his valiant parts
         Did I my soul and fortunes consecrate.
         So that, dear lords, if I be left behind,
         A moth of peace, and he go to the war,
         The rites for which I love him are bereft me,
         And I a heavy interim shall support
         By his dear absence. Let me go with him.   260

Oth.   Let her have your voices.
         Vouch with me, heaven, I therefore beg it not,
         To please the palate of my appetite;
         Nor to comply with heat—the young affects
         In me defunct—and proper satisfaction;
         But to be free and bounteous to her mind:
         And heaven defend your good souls, that you
                    think
         I will your serious and great business scant
         For she is with me. No, when light-wing'd toys
         Of feather'd Cupid seel with wanton dullness   270
         My speculative and officed instruments,
         That my disports corrupt and taint my business,
         Let housewives make a skillet of my helm,
         And all indign and base adversities
         Make head against my estimation!

Duke. Be it as you shall privately determine,
　　Either for her stay or going: the affair cries haste,
　　And speed must answer 't; you must hence
　　　　to-night.

Des. To-night, my lord?

Duke. 　　　　　This night.

Oth. 　　　　　　With all my heart.

Duke. At nine i' the morning here we'll meet again.　　280
　　Othello, leave some officer behind,
　　And he shall our commission bring to you;
　　With such things else of quality and respect
　　As doth import you.

Oth. 　　　　So please your grace, my ancient;
　　A man he is of honesty and trust:
　　To his conveyance I assign my wife,
　　With what else needful your good grace shall think
　　To be sent after me.

Duke. 　　　　Let it be so.
　　Good night to every one. [*To Brab.*] And, noble
　　　　signior,
　　If virtue no delighted beauty lack,　　　　290
　　Your son-in-law is far more fair than black.

First Sen. Adieu, brave Moor; use Desdemona well.

Bra. Look to her, Moor, if thou hast eyes to see:
　　She has deceived her father, and may thee.
　　　　　[*Exeunt Duke, Senators, Officers, &c.*

Oth. My life upon her faith! Honest Iago,
　　My Desdemona must I leave to thee:
　　I prithee, let thy wife attend on her;
　　And bring them after in the best advantage.
　　Come, Desdemona; I have but an hour
　　Of love, of worldly matters and direction,　　300
　　To spend with thee: we must obey the time.
　　　　　[*Exeunt Othello and Desdemona.*

Rod. Iago!

Iago.   What say'st thou, noble heart?

Rod.   What will I do, thinkest thou?

Iago.   Why, go to bed and sleep.

Rod.   I will incontinently drown myself.

Iago.   If thou dost, I shall never love thee after.
Why, thou silly gentleman!

Rod.   It is silliness to live when to live is torment;
and then have we a prescription to die when   310
death is our physician.

Iago.   O villanous! I have looked upon the world for
four times seven years; and since I could
distinguish betwixt a benefit and an injury,
I never found man that knew how to love
himself. Ere I would say I would drown myself
for the love of a guinea-hen, I would change
my humanity with a baboon.

Rod.   What should I do? I confess it is my shame
to be so fond; but it is not in my virtue to   320
amend it.

Iago.   Virtue! a fig! 'tis in ourselves that we are thus
or thus. Our bodies are gardens; to the which
our wills are gardeners: so that if we will plant
nettles or sow lettuce, set hyssop and weed up
thyme, supply it with one gender of herbs or
distract it with many, either to have it sterile
with idleness or manured with industry, why,
the power and corrigible authority of this lies
in our wills. If the balance of our lives had not   330
one scale of reason to poise another of
sensuality, the blood and baseness of our
natures would conduct us to most preposterous
conclusions: but we have reason to cool
our raging motions, our carnal stings, our
unbitted lusts; whereof I take this, that you
call love, to be a sect or scion.

Rod. It cannot be.

Iago. It is merely a lust of the blood and a permission
of the will. Come, be a man: drown thyself!   340
drown cats and blind puppies. I have professed
me thy friend, and I confess me knit to thy
deserving with cables of perdurable toughness:
I could never better stead thee than now. Put
money in thy purse; follow thou the wars;
defeat thy favour with an usurped beard; I say,
put money in thy purse. It cannot be that
Desdemona should long continue her love to
the Moor—put money in thy purse—nor he
his to her: it was a violent commencement,   350
and thou shalt see an answerable sequestration;
put but money in thy purse. These Moors are
changeable in their wills:—fill thy purse with
money. The food that to him now is as luscious
as locusts, shall be to him shortly as bitter as
coloquintida. She must change for youth: when
she is sated with his body, she will find the error
of her choice: she must have change, she must:
therefore put money in thy purse. If thou wilt
needs damn thyself, do it a more delicate way   360
than drowning. Make all the money thou canst:
if sanctimony and a frail vow betwixt an erring
barbarian and a supersubtle Venetian be not too
hard for my wits and all the tribe of hell, thou
shalt enjoy her; therefore make money. A pox
of drowning thyself! it is clean out of the way:
seek thou rather to be hanged in compassing thy
joy than to be drowned and go without her.

Rod. Wilt thou be fast to my hopes, if I depend on
the issue?   370

Iago. Thou art sure of me: go, make money: I have
told thee often, and I re-tell thee again and
again, I hate the Moor: my cause is hearted;
thine hath no less reason. Let us be conjunctive
in our revenge against him: if thou canst
cuckold him, thou dost thyself a pleasure, me

a sport. There are many events in the womb of
time, which will be delivered. Traverse; go;
provide thy money. We will have more of this
to-morrow. Adieu.   380

Rod. Where shall we meet i' the morning?

Iago. At my lodging.

Rod. I'll be with thee betimes.

Iago. Go to; farewell. Do you hear, Roderigo?

Rod. What say you?

Iago. No more of drowning, do you hear?

Rod. I am changed: I'll go sell all my land.   [*Exit.*

Iago. Thus do I ever make my fool my purse;
    For I mine own gain'd knowledge should
             profane,   390
    If I would time expend with such a snipe
    But for my sport and profit. I hate the Moor;
    And it is thought abroad that 'twixt my sheets
    He has done my office: I know not if 't be true;
    But I for mere suspicion in that kind
    Will do as if for surety. He holds me well;
    The better shall my purpose work on him.
    Cassio's a proper man: let me see now;
    To get his place, and to plume up my will
    In double knavery—How, how?—Let's see:—   400
    After some time, to abuse Othello's ear
    That he is too familiar with his wife.
    He hath a person and a smooth dispose
    To be suspected; framed to make women false.
    The Moor is of a free and open nature,
    That thinks men honest that but seem to be so;
    And will as tenderly be led by the nose
    As asses are.
    I have 't. It is engender'd. Hell and night
    Must bring this monstrous birth to the world's
             light.   [*Exit.*   410

ACT SECOND
SCENE I

A sea-port in Cyprus. An open place near the quay.

Enter Montano and two Gentlemen.

Mon. What from the cape can you discern at sea?

First Gent. Nothing at all: it is a high-wrought flood;
  I cannot, 'twixt the heaven and the main,
  Descry a sail.

Mon. Methinks the wind hath spoke aloud at land;
  A fuller blast ne'er shook our battlements:
  If it hath ruffian'd so upon the sea,
  What ribs of oak, when mountains melt on them,
  Can hold the mortise? What shall we hear of this?

Sec. Gent. A segregation of the Turkish fleet: 10
  For do but stand upon the foaming shore,
  The chidden billow seems to pelt the clouds;
  The wind-shaked surge, with high and
       monstrous mane,
  Seems to cast water on the burning bear,
  And quench the guards of the ever-fixed pole:
  I never did like molestation view
  On the enchafed flood.

Mon.   If that the Turkish fleet
  Be not enshelter'd and embay'd, they are drown'd;
  It is impossible to bear it out.

Enter a third Gentleman.

Third Gent. News, lads! our wars are done.   20
  The desperate tempest hath so bang'd the Turks,
  That their designment halts: a noble ship of Venice
  Hath seen a grievous wreck and sufferance
  On most part of their fleet.

Mon. How! is this true?

Third Gent.   The ship is here put in.
A Veronesa; Michael Cassio,
Lieutenant to the warlike Moor Othello,
Is come on shore: the Moor himself at sea,
And is in full commission here for Cyprus.

Mon. I am glad on 't; 'tis a worthy governor.   30

Third Gent. But this same Cassio, though he speak of
                    comfort
Touching the Turkish loss, yet he looks sadly
And prays the Moor be safe; for they were parted
With foul and violent tempest.

Mon.   Pray heavens he be;
For I have served him, and the man commands
Like a full soldier. Let's to the seaside, ho!
As well to see the vessel that's come in
As to throw out our eyes for brave Othello,
Even till we make the main and the aerial blue
An indistinct regard.

Third Gent.   Come, let's do so;   40
For every minute is expectancy
Of more arrivance.

Enter Cassio.

Cas. Thanks, you the valiant of this warlike isle,
That so approve the Moor! O, let the heavens
Give him defence against the elements,
For I have lost him on a dangerous sea.

Mon. Is he well shipp'd?

Cas. His bark is stoutly timber'd, and his pilot
Of very expert and approved allowance;
Therefore my hopes, not surfeited to death,   50
Stand in bold cure.
                    [*A cry within*: 'A sail, a sail, a sail!'

Enter a fourth Gentleman.

Cas. What noise?

Fourth Gent. The town is empty; on the brow o' the sea
    Stand ranks of people, and they cry 'A sail!'

Cas. My hopes do shape him for the governor.

                                                          [*Guns heard.*

Sec. Gent. They do discharge their shot of courtesy:
    Our friends at least.

Cas.   I pray you, sir, go forth,
    And give us truth who 'tis that is arrived.

Sec. Gent. I shall.   [*Exit.*

Mon. But, good lieutenant, is your general wived?   60

Cas. Most fortunately: he hath achieved a maid
    That paragons description and wild fame;
    One that excels the quirks of blazoning pens,
    And in the essential vesture of creation
    Does tire the ingener.

Re-enter second Gentleman.

                        How now! who has put in?

Sec. Gent. 'Tis one Iago, ancient to the general.

Cas. He has had most favourable and happy speed:
    Tempests themselves, high seas, and howling
                winds,
    The gutter'd rocks, and congregated sands,
    Traitors ensteep'd to clog the guiltless keel,   70
    As having sense of beauty, do omit
    Their mortal natures, letting go safely by
    The divine Desdemona.

Mon.   What is she?

Cas. She that I spake of, our great captain's captain,
    Left in the conduct of the bold Iago;
    Whose footing here anticipates our thoughts
    A se'nnight's speed. Great Jove, Othello guard,
    And swell his sail with thine own powerful breath,
    That he may bless this bay with his tall ship,
    Make love's quick pants in Desdemona's arms,   80

Give renew'd fire to our extinct spirits,
And bring all Cyprus comfort.

Enter Desdemona, Emilia, Iago, Roderigo, and Attendants.

O, behold,
The riches of the ship is come on shore!
Ye men of Cyprus, let her have your knees.
Hail to thee, lady! and the grace of heaven,
Before, behind thee, and on every hand,
Enwheel thee round!

Des.   I thank you, valiant Cassio.
What tidings can you tell me of my lord?

Cas.   He is not yet arrived: nor know I aught
But that he's well and will be shortly here.   90

Des.   O, but I fear—How lost you company?

Cas.   The great contention of the sea and skies
Parted our fellowship—But, hark! a sail.
                    [*A cry within:* 'A sail, a sail!' *Guns heard.*

Sec. Gent. They give their greeting to the citadel:
This likewise is a friend.

Cas.   See for the news.
                    [*Exit Gentleman.*
Good ancient, you are welcome. [*To Emilia*]
                    Welcome, mistress:
Let it not gall your patience, good Iago,
That I extend my manners; 'tis my breeding
That gives me this bold show of courtesy.   100
                    [*Kissing her.*

Iago.   Sir, would she give you so much of her lips
As of her tongue she oft bestows on me,
You'ld have enough.

Des.   Alas, she has no speech.

Iago.   In faith, too much;
I find it still when I have list to sleep:
Marry, before your ladyship, I grant,

She puts her tongue a little in her heart
And chides with thinking.

Emil. You have little cause to say so.

Iago. Come on, come on; you are pictures out of doors,   110
Bells in your parlours, wild-cats in your kitchens,
Saints in your injuries, devils being offended,
Players in your housewifery, and housewives in
         your beds.

Des. O, fie upon thee, slanderer!

Iago. Nay, it is true, or else I am a Turk:
You rise to play, and go to bed to work.

Emil. You shall not write my praise.

Iago.   No, let me not.

Des. What wouldst thou write of me, if thou shouldst
         praise me?

Iago. O gentle lady, do not put me to 't;
For I am nothing if not critical.   120

Des. Come on, assay—There's one gone to the harbour?

Iago. Ay, madam.

Des. I am not merry; but I do beguile
The thing I am by seeming otherwise.
Come, how wouldst thou praise me?

Iago. I am about it; but indeed my invention
Comes from my pate as birdlime does from frize;
It plucks out brains and all: but my Muse labours,
And thus she is deliver'd.
If she be fair and wise, fairness and wit,   130
The one's for use, the other useth it.

Des. Well praised! How if she be black and witty?

Iago. If she be black, and thereto have a wit,
She'll find a white that shall her blackness fit.

Des. Worse and worse.

Emil. How if fair and foolish?

Iago. She never yet was foolish that was fair;
For even her folly help'd her to an heir.

Des. These are old fond paradoxes to make fools
laugh i' the alehouse. What miserable praise   140
hast thou for her that's foul and foolish?

Iago. There's none so foul, and foolish thereunto,
But does foul pranks which fair and wise ones do.

Des. O heavy ignorance! thou praisest the worst
best. But what praise couldst thou bestow on a
deserving woman indeed, one that in the
authority of her merit did justly put on the
vouch of very malice itself?

Iago. She that was ever fair and never proud,
Had tongue at will and yet was never loud,   150
Never lack'd gold and yet went never gay,
Fled from her wish and yet said 'Now I may;'
She that, being anger'd, her revenge being nigh,
Bade her wrong stay and her displeasure fly;
She that in wisdom never was so frail
To change the cod's head for the salmon's tail;
She that could think and ne'er disclose her mind,
See suitors following and not look behind;
She was a wight, if ever such wight were,—

Des. To do what?   160

Iago. To suckle fools and chronicle small beer.

Des. O most lame and impotent conclusion! Do not
learn of him, Emilia, though he be thy
husband. How say you, Cassio? is he not a
most profane and liberal counsellor?

Cas. He speaks home, madam: you may relish him
more in the soldier than in the scholar.

Iago. [*Aside*] He takes her by the palm: ay, well said,
whisper: with as little a web as this will I

ensnare as great a fly as Cassio. Ay, smile   170
upon her, do; I will gyve thee in thine own
courtship. You say true; 'tis so, indeed: if
such tricks as these strip you out of your
lieutenantry, it had been better you had not
kissed your three fingers so oft, which now
again you are most apt to play the sir in. Very
good; well kissed! an excellent courtesy! 'tis so,
indeed. Yet again your fingers to your lips?
would they were clyster-pipes for your sake!—
[*Trumpet within.*] The Moor! I know his trumpet.   180

Cas.   'Tis truly so.

Des.   Let's meet him and receive him.

Cas.   Lo, where he comes!

Enter Othello and Attendants.

Oth.   O my fair warrior!

Des.   My dear Othello!

Oth.   It gives me wonder great as my content
To see you here before me. O my soul's joy!
If after every tempest come such calms,
May the winds blow till they have waken'd death!
And let the labouring bark climb hills of seas
Olympus-high, and duck again as low   190
As hell's from heaven! If it were now to die,
'Twere now to be most happy; for I fear,
My soul hath her content so absolute
That not another comfort like to this
Succeeds in unknown fate.

Des.   The heavens forbid
But that our loves and comforts should increase,
Even as our days do grow!

Oth.   Amen to that, sweet powers!
I cannot speak enough of this content;
It stops me here; it is too much of joy:
And this, and this, the greatest discords be   200

62

[Kissing her.

That e'er our hearts shall make!

Iago.   *[Aside]* O, you are well tuned now!
But I'll set down the pegs that make this music,
As honest as I am.

Oth.   Come, let us to the castle.
News, friends; our wars are done, the Turks are
          drown'd.
How does my old acquaintance of this isle?
Honey, you shall be well desired in Cyprus;
I have found great love amongst them. O my sweet,
I prattle out of fashion, and I dote
In mine own comforts. I prithee, good Iago,
Go to the bay, and disembark my coffers: 210
Bring thou the master to the citadel;
He is a good one, and his worthiness
Does challenge much respect. Come, Desdemona,
Once more well met at Cyprus.
          [Exeunt all but Iago and Roderigo.

Iago.   Do thou meet me presently at the harbour.
Come hither. If thou be'st valiant—as, they say,
base men being in love have then a nobility in
their natures more than is native to them—list
me. The lieutenant to-night watches on the
court of guard. First, I must tell thee this: 220
Desdemona is directly in love with him.

Rod.   With him! why, 'tis not possible.

Iago.   Lay thy finger thus, and let thy soul be
instructed. Mark me with what violence she
first loved the Moor, but for bragging and
telling her fantastical lies: and will she love him
still for prating? let not thy discreet heart think
it. Her eye must be fed; and what delight shall
she have to look on the devil? When the blood
is made dull with the act of sport, there should   230
be, again to inflame it and to give satiety a fresh
appetite, loveliness in favour, sympathy in years,
manners and beauties; all which the Moor is

defective in: now, for want of these required
conveniences, her delicate tenderness will find
itself abused, begin to heave the gorge, disrelish
and abhor the Moor; very nature will instruct
her in it and compel her to some second choice.
Now, sir, this granted—as it is a most pregnant
and unforced position—who stands so eminently   240
in the degree of this fortune as Cassio does?
a knave very voluble; no further conscionable
than in putting on the mere form of civil and
humane seeming, for the better compassing of
his salt and most hidden loose affection? why,
none; why, none: a slipper and subtle knave;
a finder out of occasions; that has an eye can
stamp and counterfeit advantages, though true
advantage never present itself: a devilish knave!
Besides, the knave is handsome, young, and hath   250
all those requisites in him that folly and green
minds look after: a pestilent complete knave;
and the woman hath found him already.

Rod. I cannot believe that in her; she's full of most
blest condition.

Iago. Blest fig's-end! the wine she drinks is made of
grapes: if she had been blest, she would never
have loved the Moor: blest pudding! Didst
thou not see her paddle with the palm of his
hand? didst not mark that?   260

Rod. Yes, that I did; but that was but
courtesy.

Iago. Lechery, by this hand; an index and obscure
prologue to the history of lust and foul
thoughts. They met so near with their lips that
their breaths embraced together. Villanous
thoughts, Roderigo! when these mutualities so
marshal the way, hard at hand comes the master
and main exercise, the incorporate conclusion:
pish! But, sir, be you ruled by me: I have   270
brought you from Venice. Watch you to-night;

for the command, I'll lay 't upon you: Cassio
knows you not: I'll not be far from you: do you
find some occasion to anger Cassio, either by
speaking too loud, or tainting his discipline, or
from what other course you please, which the
time shall more favourably minister.

Rod. Well.

Iago. Sir, he is rash and very sudden in choler, and
haply may strike at you: provoke him, that he   280
may; for even out of that will I cause these of
Cyprus to mutiny; whose qualification shall
come into no true taste again but by the
displanting of Cassio. So shall you have a shorter
journey to your desires by the means I shall then
have to prefer them, and the impediment most
profitably removed, without the which there
were no expectation of our prosperity.

Rod. I will do this, if I can bring it to any
opportunity.   290

Iago. I warrant thee. Meet me by and by at the
citadel: I must fetch his necessaries ashore.
Farewell.

Rod. Adieu.   [*Exit.*

Iago. That Cassio loves her, I do well believe it;
That she loves him, 'tis apt and of great credit:
The Moor, howbeit that I endure him not,
Is of a constant, loving, noble nature;
And I dare think he'll prove to Desdemona
A most dear husband. Now, I do love her too,   300
Not out of absolute lust, though peradventure
I stand accountant for as great a sin,
But partly led to diet my revenge,
For that I do suspect the lusty Moor
Hath leap'd into my seat: the thought whereof
Doth like a poisonous mineral gnaw my inwards;
And nothing can or shall content my soul
Till I am even'd with him, wife for wife;

65

Or failing so, yet that I put the Moor
At least into a jealousy so strong   310
That judgement cannot cure. Which thing to do,
If this poor trash of Venice, whom I trash
For his quick hunting, stand the putting on,
I'll have our Michael Cassio on the hip,
Abuse him to the Moor in the rank garb;
For I fear Cassio with my night-cap too;
Make the Moor thank me, love me and reward me,
For making him egregiously an ass
And practising upon his peace and quiet
Even to madness. 'Tis here, but yet confused: 320
Knavery's plain face is never seen till used.   [*Exit.*

SCENE II

A street.

Enter a Herald with a proclamation; People
following.

Her.   It is Othello's pleasure, our noble and valiant
general, that upon certain tidings now arrived,
importing the mere perdition of the Turkish
fleet, every man put himself into triumph;
some to dance, some to make bonfires, each
man to what sport and revels his addiction
leads him: for, besides these beneficial news, it
is the celebration of his nuptial. So much was
his pleasure should be proclaimed. All offices
are open, and there is full liberty of feasting
from this present hour of five till the bell have   10
told eleven. Heaven bless the isle of Cyprus
and our noble general Othello!   [*Exeunt.*

SCENE III

A hall in the castle.

Enter Othello, Desdemona, Cassio, and Attendants.

Oth.   Good Michael, look you to the guard to-night:
Let's teach ourselves that honourable stop,
Not to outsport discretion.

Cas.   Iago hath direction what to do;
But notwithstanding with my personal eye
Will I look to 't.

Oth.   Iago is most honest.
Michael, good night: to-morrow with your earliest
Let me have speech with you. Come, my dear love,
The purchase made, the fruits are to ensue;
That profit's yet to come 'tween me and you.   10
Good night.

   [*Exeunt Othello, Desdemona, and Attendants.*

Enter Iago.

Cas.   Welcome, Iago; we must to the watch.

Iago.   Not this hour, lieutenant; 'tis not yet ten o' the
clock. Our general cast us thus early for the
love of his Desdemona; who, let us not
therefore blame: he hath not yet made wanton
the night with her, and she is sport for Jove.

Cas.   She's a most exquisite lady.

Iago.   And, I'll warrant her, full of game.

Cas.   Indeed she's a most fresh and delicate   20
creature.

Iago.   What an eye she has! methinks it sounds a parley
to provocation.

Cas.   An inviting eye; and yet methinks right
modest.

Iago.   And when she speaks, is it not an alarum
to love?

Cas.   She is indeed perfection.

Iago.   Well, happiness to their sheets! Come,
lieutenant, I have a stoup of wine; and here   30
without are a brace of Cyprus gallants that
would fain have a measure to the health of
black Othello.

Cas.   Not to-night, good Iago: I have very poor and
unhappy brains for drinking: I could well wish
courtesy would invent some other custom of
entertainment.

Iago.   O, they are our friends; but one cup: I'll drink
for you.

Cas.   I have drunk but one cup to-night, and that   40
was craftily qualified too, and behold what
innovation it makes here: I am unfortunate in
the infirmity, and dare not task my weakness
with any more.

Iago.   What, man: 'tis a night of revels: the gallants
desire it.

Cas.   Where are they?

Iago.   Here at the door; I pray you, call them in.

Cas.   I'll do 't; but it dislikes me.   [*Exit.*

Iago.   If I can fasten but one cup upon him,   50
With that which he hath drunk to-night already,
He'll be as full of quarrel and offence
As my young mistress' dog. Now my sick fool
          Roderigo,
Whom love hath turn'd almost the wrong
          side out,
To Desdemona hath to-night caroused

Potations pottle-deep; and he's to watch:
Three lads of Cyprus, noble swelling spirits,
That hold their honours in a wary distance,
The very elements of this warlike isle,
Have I to-night fluster'd with flowing cups,   60
And they watch too. Now, 'mongst this flock of
      drunkards,
Am I to put our Cassio in some action
That may offend the isle. But here they come:
If consequence do but approve my dream,
My boat sails freely, both with wind and stream.

Re-enter Cassio; with him Montano and Gentlemen;
Servants following with wine.

Cas.   'Fore God, they have given me a rouse already.

Mon.   Good faith, a little one; not past a pint, as I am
      a soldier.

Iago.   Some wine, ho!   70
      [*Sings*] And let me the canakin clink, clink
           And let me the canakin clink:
              A soldier's a man;
              A life's but a span;
           Why then let a soldier drink.
      Some wine, boys!

Cas.   'Fore God, an excellent song.

Iago.   I learned it in England, where indeed they are
      most potent in potting: your Dane, your
      German, and your swag-bellied Hollander,—   80
      Drink, ho!—are nothing to your English.

Cas.   Is your Englishman so expert in his
      drinking?

Iago.   Why, he drinks you with facility your Dane
      dead drunk; he sweats not to overthrow your
      Almain; he gives your Hollander a vomit ere
      the next pottle can be filled.

Cas.   To the health of our general!

Mon. I am for it, lieutenant, and I'll do you
justice.   90

Iago. O sweet England!
[*Sings*] King Stephen was a worthy peer,
      His breeches cost him but a crown;
He held them sixpence all too dear,
      With that he call'd the tailor lown.
He was a wight of high renown,
      And thou art but of low degree:
'Tis pride that pulls the country down;
      Then take thine auld cloak about thee.
Some wine, ho!   100

Cas. Why, this is a more exquisite song than the
other.

Iago. Will you hear't again?

Cas. No; for I hold him to be unworthy of his place
that does those things. Well: God's above all;
and there be souls must be saved, and there be
souls must not be saved.

Iago. It's true, good lieutenant.

Cas. For mine own part—no offence to the
general, nor any man of quality—I hope to be   110
saved.

Iago. And so do I too, lieutenant.

Cas. Ay, but, by your leave, not before me; the
lieutenant is to be saved before the ancient.
Let's have no more of this; let's to our affairs.
God forgive us our sins! Gentlemen, let's look
to our business. Do not think, gentlemen, I am
drunk: this is my ancient: this is my right hand,
and this is my left. I am not drunk now; I can
stand well enough, and speak well enough.   120

All. Excellent well.

Cas. Why, very well then; you must not think then
that I am drunk.   [*Exit.*

Mon. To the platform, masters; come, let's set the
watch.

Iago. You see this fellow that is gone before;
He is a soldier fit to stand by Cæsar
And give direction: and do but see his vice;
'Tis to his virtue a just equinox,
The one as long as the other: 'tis pity of him.   130
I fear the trust Othello puts him in
On some odd time of his infirmity
Will shake this island.

Mon.   But is he often thus?

Iago. 'Tis evermore the prologue to his sleep:
He'll watch the horologe a double set,
If drink rock not his cradle.

Mon.   It were well
 The general were put in mind of it.
Perhaps he sees it not, or his good nature
Prizes the virtue that appears in Cassio
And looks not on his evils: is not this true?   140

Enter Roderigo.

Iago. [*Aside to him*] How now, Roderigo!
I pray you, after the lieutenant; go.

                              [*Exit Roderigo.*

Mon. And 'tis great pity that the noble Moor
Should hazard such a place as his own second
With one of an ingraft infirmity:
It were an honest action to say
So to the Moor.

Iago.   Not I, for this fair island:
I do love Cassio well, and would do much
To cure him of this evil:—But, hark! what noise?
                    [*A cry within*: 'Help! help!'

Re-enter Cassio, driving in Roderigo.

Cas. 'Zounds! you rogue! you rascal!

Mon.   What's the matter, lieutenant?   150

71

Cas. A knave teach me my duty! But I'll beat the
knave into a wicker bottle.

Rod. Beat me!

Cas.   Dost thou prate, rogue?   [*Striking Roderigo.*

Mon. Nay, good lieutenant; I pray you, sir, hold your hand.

Cas. Let me go, sir, or I'll knock you o'er the mazzard.

Mon. Come, come, you're drunk.

Cas.   Drunk!   [*They fight.*

Iago. [*Aside to Roderigo*] Away, I say; go out and cry
                a mutiny.   [*Exit Roderigo.*
Nay, good lieutenant! God's will, gentlemen!
Help, ho!—Lieutenant,—sir,—Montano,—sir;—
Help, masters!—Here's a goodly watch indeed!
                                [*A bell rings.*
Who's that that rings the bell?—Diablo, ho!   161
The town will rise: God's will, lieutenant, hold;
You will be shamed for ever.

Re-enter Othello and Attendants.

Oth.   What is the matter here?

Mon. 'Zounds, I bleed still; I am hurt to the death.   [*Faints.*

Oth. Hold, for your lives!

Iago. Hold, ho! Lieutenant,—sir,—Montano,—
                gentlemen,—
Have you forgot all sense of place and duty?
Hold! the general speaks to you; hold, hold, for
                shame!

Oth. Why, how now, ho! from whence ariseth this?
Are we turn'd Turks, and to ourselves do that   170
Which heaven hath forbid the Ottomites?
For Christian shame, put by this barbarous brawl:
He that stirs next to carve for his own rage
Holds his soul light; he dies upon his motion.
Silence that dreadful bell: it frights the isle

From her propriety. What is the matter, masters?
Honest Iago, that look'st dead with grieving,
Speak, who began this? on thy love, I charge thee.

Iago.   I do not know: friends all, but now, even now,
In quarter, and in terms like bride and groom   180
Divesting them for bed; and then, but now,
As if some planet had unwitted men,
Swords out, and tilting one at other's breast,
In opposition bloody. I cannot speak
Any beginning to this peevish odds;
And would in action glorious I had lost
Those legs that brought me to a part of it!

Oth.   How comes it, Michael, you are thus forgot?

Cas.   I pray you, pardon me; I cannot speak.

Oth.   Worthy Montano, you were wont be civil;   190
The gravity and stillness of your youth
The world hath noted, and your name is great
In mouths of wisest censure: what's the matter,
That you unlace your reputation thus,
And spend your rich opinion for the name
Of a night-brawler? give me answer to it.

Mon.   Worthy Othello, I am hurt to danger:
Your officer, Iago, can inform you—
While I spare speech, which something now
             offends me—
Of all that I do know: nor know I aught   200
By me that's said or done amiss this night;
Unless self-charity be sometimes a vice,
And to defend ourselves it be a sin
When violence assails us.

Oth.   Now, by heaven,
My blood begins my safer guides to rule,
And passion, having my best judgement collied,
Assays to lead the way: if I once stir,
Or do but lift this arm, the best of you
Shall sink in my rebuke. Give me to know
How this foul rout began, who set it on,   210

And he that is approved in this offence,
Though he had twinn'd with me, both at a birth,
Shall lose me. What! in a town of war,
Yet wild, the people's hearts brimful of fear,
To manage private and domestic quarrel,
In night, and on the court and guard of safety!
'Tis monstrous. Iago, who began 't?

Mon. If partially affined, or leagued in office,
Thou dost deliver more or less than truth,
Thou art no soldier.

Iago.   Touch me not so near: 220
I had rather have this tongue cut from my mouth
Than it should do offence to Michael Cassio;
Yet, I persuade myself, to speak the truth
Shall nothing wrong him. Thus it is, general.
Montano and myself being in speech,
There comes a fellow crying out for help,
And Cassio following him with determined
                  sword,
To execute upon him. Sir, this gentleman
Steps in to Cassio and entreats his pause:
Myself the crying fellow did pursue,   230
Lest by his clamour—as it so fell out—
The town might fall in fright: he, swift of foot,
Outran my purpose; and I return'd the rather
For that I heard the clink and fall of swords,
And Cassio high in oath; which till to-night
I ne'er might say before. When I came back—
For this was brief—I found them close together,
At blow and thrust; even as again they were
When you yourself did part them.
More of this matter cannot I report: 240
But men are men; the best sometimes forget:
Though Cassio did some little wrong to him,
As men in rage strike those that wish them best,
Yet surely Cassio, I believe, received
From him that fled some strange indignity,
Which patience could not pass.

Oth.   I know, Iago,

Thy honesty and love doth mince this matter,
Making it light to Cassio. Cassio, I love thee;
But never more be officer of mine.

Re-enter Desdemona, attended.

Look, if my gentle love be not raised up!   250
I'll make thee an example.

Des.   What's the matter?

Oth.   All's well now, sweeting; come away to bed.
Sir, for your hurts, myself will be your surgeon:
[*To Montano, who is led off.*] Lead him off.
Iago, look with care about the town,
And silence those whom this vile brawl distracted.
Come, Desdemona: 'tis the soldiers' life
To have their balmy slumbers waked with strife.
                              [*Exeunt all but Iago and Cassio.*

Iago. What, are you hurt, lieutenant?

Cas.   Ay, past all surgery.   260

Iago. Marry, heaven forbid!

Cas.   Reputation, reputation, reputation! O, I have
lost my reputation! I have lost the immortal
part of myself, and what remains is bestial.
My reputation, Iago, my reputation!

Iago. As I am an honest man, I thought you had
received some bodily wound; there is more
sense in that than in reputation. Reputation is
an idle and most false imposition; oft got
without merit and lost without deserving: you   270
have lost no reputation at all, unless you repute
yourself such a loser. What, man! there are ways
to recover the general again: you are but now
cast in his mood, a punishment more in policy
than in malice; even so as one would beat his
offenceless dog to affright an imperious lion:
sue to him again, and he's yours.

Cas.   I will rather sue to be despised than to deceive

so good a commander with so slight, so
drunken, and so indiscreet an officer. Drunk?   280
and speak parrot? and squabble? swagger? swear?
and discourse fustian with one's own shadow?
O thou invisible spirit of wine, if thou hast no
name to be known by, let us call thee devil!

Iago. What was he that you followed with your
sword? What had he done to you?

Cas. I know not.

Iago. Is 't possible?

Cas. I remember a mass of things, but nothing
distinctly; a quarrel, but nothing wherefore.   290
O God, that men should put an enemy in their
mouths to steal away their brains! that we
should, with joy, pleasance, revel and applause,
transform ourselves into beasts!

Iago. Why, but you are now well enough: how came
you thus recovered?

Cas. It hath pleased the devil drunkenness to give
place to the devil wrath: one unperfectness
shows me another, to make me frankly despise
myself.   300

Iago. Come, you are too severe a moraler: as the
time, the place, and the condition of this
country stands, I could heartily wish this had
not befallen; but since it is as it is, mend it for
your own good.

Cas. I will ask him for my place again; he shall
tell me I am a drunkard! Had I as many
mouths as Hydra, such an answer would stop
them all. To be now a sensible man, by and
by a fool, and presently a beast! O strange!   310
Every inordinate cup is unblest, and the
ingredient is a devil.

Iago. Come, come, good wine is a good familiar
creature, if it be well used: exclaim no more

against it. And, good lieutenant, I think you
think I love you.

Cas.   I have well approved it, sir. I drunk!

Iago.   You or any man living may be drunk at some
time, man. I'll tell you what you shall do.
Our general's wife is now the general. I may say   320
so in this respect, for that he hath devoted and
given up himself to the contemplation, mark
and denotement of her parts and graces: confess
yourself freely to her; importune her help to
put you in your place again: she is of so free, so
kind, so apt, so blessed a disposition, she holds
it a vice in her goodness not to do more than
she is requested: this broken joint between you
and her husband entreat her to splinter; and, my
fortunes against any lay worth naming, this crack of   330
your love shall grow stronger than it was before.

Cas.   You advise me well.

Iago.   I protest, in the sincerity of love and honest
kindness.

Cas.   I think it freely; and betimes in the morning
I will beseech the virtuous Desdemona to
undertake for me: I am desperate of my
fortunes if they check me here.

Iago.   You are in the right. Good night, lieutenant;
I must to the watch.   340

Cas.   Good night, honest Iago.   [*Exit.*

Iago.   And what's he then that says I play the villain?
When this advice is free I give and honest,
Probal to thinking, and indeed the course
To win the Moor again? For 'tis most easy
The inclining Desdemona to subdue
In any honest suit. She's framed as fruitful
As the free elements. And then for her
To win the Moor, were 't to renounce his baptism,
All seals and symbols of redeemed sin,   350

77

His soul is so enfetter'd to her love,
That she may make, unmake, do what she list,
Even as her appetite shall play the god
With his weak function. How am I then a villain
To counsel Cassio to this parallel course,
Directly to his good? Divinity of hell!
When devils will the blackest sins put on,
They do suggest at first with heavenly shows,
As I do now: for whiles this honest fool
Plies Desdemona to repair his fortunes,   360
And she for him pleads strongly to the Moor,
I'll pour this pestilence into his ear,
That she repeals him for her body's lust;
And by how much she strives to do him good,
She shall undo her credit with the Moor.
So will I turn her virtue into pitch;
And out of her own goodness make the net
That shall enmesh them all.

Enter Roderigo.

                         How now, Roderigo!

Rod.   I do follow here in the chase, not like a hound
that hunts, but one that fills up the cry. My   370
money is almost spent; I have been to-night
exceedingly well cudgelled; and I think the
issue will be, I shall have so much experience
for my pains; and so, with no money at all and
a little more wit, return again to Venice.

Iago.   How poor are they that have not patience!
What wound did ever heal but by degrees?
Thou know'st we work by wit and not by
           witchcraft,
And wit depends on dilatory time.
Does't not go well? Cassio hath beaten thee,   380
And thou by that small hurt hast cashier'd Cassio:
Though other things grow fair against the sun,
Yet fruits that blossom first will first be ripe:
Content thyself awhile. By the mass, 'tis morning;
Pleasure and action make the hours seem short.

Retire thee; go where thou art billeted:
Away, I say; thou shalt know more hereafter:
Nay, get thee gone. [*Exit Rod.*] Two things are
        to be done:
My wife must move for Cassio to her mistress;
I'll set her on;   390
Myself the while to draw the Moor apart,
And bring him jump when he may Cassio find
Soliciting his wife: ay, that's the way;
Dull not device by coldness and delay.   [*Exit.*

ACT THIRD
SCENE I

Before the castle.

Enter Cassio and some Musicians.

Cas.   Masters, play here; I will content your pains;
      Something that's brief; and bid 'Good morrow,
           general.'   [*Music.*

Enter Clown.

Clo.   Why, masters, have your instruments been in
      Naples, that they speak i' the nose thus?

First Mus. How, sir, how?

Clo.   Are these, I pray you, wind-instruments?

First Mus. Ay, marry, are they, sir.

Clo.   O, thereby hangs a tail.

First Mus. Whereby hangs a tale, sir?

Clo.   Marry, sir, by many a wind-instrument that   10
      I know. But, masters, here's money for you: and
      the general so likes your music, that he desires

you, for love's sake, to make no more noise
with it.

First Mus. Well, sir, we will not.

Clo. If you have any music that may not be heard,
to 't again: but, as they say, to hear music the
general does not greatly care.

First Mus. We have none such, sir.

Clo. Then put up your pipes in your bag, for I'll   20
away: go; vanish into air; away!

                                              [*Exeunt Musicians.*

Cas. Dost thou hear, my honest friend?

Clo. No, I hear not your honest friend; I hear
you.

Cas. Prithee, keep up thy quillets. There's a poor
piece of gold for thee: if the gentlewoman that
attends the general's wife be stirring, tell her
there's one Cassio entreats her a little favour of
speech: wilt thou do this?

Clo. She is stirring, sir: if she will stir hither, I shall   30
seem to notify unto her.

Cas. Do, good my friend.   [*Exit Clown.*

Enter Iago.

          In happy time, Iago.

Iago. You have not been a-bed, then?

Cas. Why, no; the day had broke
Before we parted. I have made bold, Iago,
To send in to your wife: my suit to her
Is, that she will to virtuous Desdemona
Procure me some access.

Iago.   I'll send her to you presently;
And I'll devise a mean to draw the Moor
Out of the way, that your converse and business   40
May be more free.

Cas. I humbly thank you for 't. [*Exit Iago.*] I never
        knew
    A Florentine more kind and honest.

Enter Emilia.

Emil. Good morrow, good lieutenant: I am sorry
    For your displeasure; but all will sure be well.
    The general and his wife are talking of it,
    And she speaks for you stoutly: the Moor replies,
    That he you hurt is of great fame in Cyprus
    And great affinity, and that in wholesome
              wisdom
    He might not but refuse you; but he protests
          he loves you,   50
    And needs no other suitor but his likings
    To take the safest occasion by the front
    To bring you in again.

Cas.   Yet, I beseech you,
    If you think fit, or that it may be done,
    Give me advantage of some brief discourse
    With Desdemona alone.

Emil.   Pray you, come in:
    I will bestow you where you shall have time
    To speak your bosom freely.

Cas.   I am much bound to you.
                        [*Exeunt.*

SCENE II

A room in the castle.

Enter Othello, Iago, and Gentlemen.

Oth. These letters give, Iago, to the pilot;
    And by him do my duties to the senate:

That done, I will be walking on the works:
Repair there to me.

Iago.   Well, my good lord, I'll do 't.

Oth. This fortification, gentlemen, shall we see 't?

Gent. We'll wait upon your lordship.   [*Exeunt.*

SCENE III

A room in the castle.

Enter Desdemona, Cassio, and Emilia.

Des. Be thou assured, good Cassio, I will do
All my abilities in thy behalf.

Emil. Good madam, do: I warrant it grieves my husband
As if the case were his.

Des. O, that's an honest fellow. Do not doubt, Cassio,
But I will have my lord and you again
As friendly as you were.

Cas.   Bounteous madam,
Whatever shall become of Michael Cassio,
He's never any thing but your true servant.

Des. I know 't: I thank you. You do love my lord: 10
You have known him long; and be you well
          assured
He shall in strangeness stand no farther off
Than in a politic distance.

Cas.   Ay, but, lady,
That policy may either last so long,
Or feed upon such nice and waterish diet,
Or breed itself so out of circumstance,
That, I being absent and my place supplied,
My general will forget my love and service.

Des.   Do not doubt that; before Emilia here
        I give thee warrant of thy place: assure thee,   20
        If I do vow a friendship, I'll perform it
        To the last article: my lord shall never rest;
        I'll watch him tame and talk him out of
                patience;
        His bed shall seem a school, his board a shrift;
        I'll intermingle every thing he does
        With Cassio's suit: therefore be merry, Cassio;
        For thy solicitor shall rather die
        Than give thy cause away.

Enter Othello and Iago, at a distance.

Emil.   Madam, here comes my lord.

Cas.   Madam, I'll take my leave.   30

Des.   Nay, stay and hear me speak.

Cas.   Madam, not now: I am very ill at ease,
        Unfit for mine own purposes.

Des.   Well, do your discretion.   *[Exit Cassio.*

Iago.   Ha! I like not that.

Oth.   What dost thou say?

Iago.   Nothing, my lord: or if—I know not what.

Oth.   Was not that Cassio parted from my wife?

Iago.   Cassio, my lord! No, sure, I cannot think it,
        That he would steal away so guilty-like,
        Seeing you coming.

Oth.   I do believe 'twas he.   40

Des.   How now, my lord!
        I have been talking with a suitor here,
        A man that languishes in your displeasure.

Oth.   Who is 't you mean?

Des.   Why, your lieutenant, Cassio. Good my lord,
        If I have any grace or power to move you,

His present reconciliation take;
For if he be not one that truly loves you,
That errs in ignorance and not in cunning,
I have no judgement in an honest face: 50
I prithee, call him back.

Oth.   Went he hence now?

Des.   Ay, sooth; so humbled,
That he hath left part of his grief with me,
To suffer with him. Good love, call him back.

Oth.   Not now, sweet Desdemona; some other time.

Des.   But shall 't be shortly?

Oth.   The sooner, sweet, for you.

Des.   Shall 't be to-night at supper?

Oth.   No, not to-night.

Des.   To-morrow dinner then?

Oth.   I shall not dine at home;
I meet the captains at the citadel.

Des.   Why then to-morrow night; or Tuesday morn;   60
On Tuesday noon, or night; on Wednesday morn:
I prithee, name the time; but let it not
Exceed three days: in faith, he's penitent;
And yet his trespass, in our common reason—
Save that, they say, the wars must make examples
Out of their best—is not almost a fault
To incur a private check. When shall he come?
Tell me, Othello: I wonder in my soul,
What you would ask me, that I should deny,
Or stand so mammering on. What! Michael
          Cassio,   70
That came a-wooing with you, and so many a
          time
When I have spoke of you dispraisingly
Hath ta'en your part; to have so much to do
To bring him in! Trust me, I could do much—

Oth. Prithee, no more: let him come when he will;
I will deny thee nothing.

Des.   Why, this is not a boon;
'Tis as I should entreat you wear your gloves,
Or feed on nourishing dishes, or keep you
      warm,
Or sue to you to do a peculiar profit
To your own person: nay, when I have a suit   80
Wherein I mean to touch your love indeed,
It shall be full of poise and difficult weight,
And fearful to be granted.

Oth.   I will deny thee nothing:
Whereon, I do beseech thee, grant me this,
To leave me but a little to myself.

Des. Shall I deny you? no: farewell, my lord.

Oth. Farewell, my Desdemona: I'll come to thee
      straight.

Des. Emilia, come. Be as your fancies teach you;
Whate'er you be, I am obedient.
                  [Exeunt Desdemona and Emilia.

Oth. Excellent wretch! Perdition catch my soul,   90
But I do love thee! and when I love thee not,
Chaos is come again.

Iago. My noble lord,—

Oth.   What dost thou say, Iago?

Iago. Did Michael Cassio, when you woo'd my lady,
Know of your love?

Oth. He did, from first to last: why dost thou ask?

Iago. But for a satisfaction of my thought;
No further harm.

Oth.   Why of thy thought, Iago?

Iago. I did not think he had been acquainted with her.

Oth. O, yes, and went between us very oft.   100

Iago. Indeed!

Oth. Indeed! ay, indeed: discern'st thou aught in that?
Is he not honest?

Iago.   Honest, my lord!

Oth. Honest! ay, honest.

Iago.   My lord, for aught I know.

Oth. What dost thou think?

Iago.   Think, my lord!

Oth. Think, my lord! By heaven, he echoes me,
As if there were some monster in his thought
Too hideous to be shown. Thou dost mean
       something:
I heard thee say even now, thou likedst not that,
When Cassio left my wife: what didst not like?   110
And when I told thee he was of my counsel
In my whole course of wooing, thou criedst
      'Indeed!'
And didst contract and purse thy brow together,
As if thou then hadst shut up in thy brain
Some horrible conceit: if thou dost love me,
Show me thy thought.

Iago. My lord, you know I love you.

Oth.   I think thou dost;
And for I know thou'rt full of love and honesty
And weigh'st thy words before thou givest them
      breath,
Therefore these stops of thine fright me the more: 120
For such things in a false disloyal knave
Are tricks of custom; but in a man that's just
They're close delations, working from the heart,
That passion cannot rule.

Iago.   For Michael Cassio,
I dare be sworn I think that he is honest.

Oth. I think so too.

Iago.   Men should be what they seem;
          Or those that be not, would they might seem
                    none!

Oth.   Certain, men should be what they seem.

Iago.   Why then I think Cassio's an honest man.

Oth.   Nay, yet there's more in this: 130
          I prithee, speak to me as to thy thinkings,
          As thou dost ruminate, and give thy worst of
                    thoughts
          The worst of words.

Iago.   Good my lord, pardon me:
          Though I am bound to every act of duty,
          I am not bound to that all slaves are free to.
          Utter my thoughts? Why, say they are vile and
                    false;
          As where's that palace whereinto foul things
          Sometimes intrude not? who has a breast so pure,
          But some uncleanly apprehensions
          Keep leets and law-days, and in session sit   140
          With meditations lawful?

Oth.   Thou dost conspire against thy friend, Iago,
          If thou but think'st him wrong'd and makest
                    his ear
          A stranger to thy thoughts.

Iago.   I do beseech you—
          Though I perchance am vicious in my guess,
          As, I confess, it is my nature's plague
          To spy into abuses, and oft my jealousy
          Shapes faults that are not—that your wisdom yet,
          From one that so imperfectly conceits,
          Would take no notice, nor build yourself a trouble   150
          Out of his scattering and unsure observance.
          It were not for your quiet nor your good,
          Nor for my manhood, honesty, or wisdom,
          To let you know my thoughts.

Oth.   What dost thou mean?

Iago. Good name in man and woman, dear my lord,
Is the immediate jewel of their souls:
Who steals my purse steals trash; 'tis
        something, nothing;
'Twas mine, 'tis his, and has been slave to
        thousands;
But he that filches from me my good name
Robs me of that which not enriches him   160
And makes me poor indeed.

Oth. By heaven, I'll know thy thoughts.

Iago. You cannot, if my heart were in your hand;
Nor shall not, whilst 'tis in my custody.

Oth. Ha!

Iago.   O, beware, my lord, of jealousy;
It is the green-eyed monster, which doth mock
The meat it feeds on: that cuckold lives in bliss
Who, certain of his fate, loves not his wronger;
But, O, what damned minutes tells he o'er
Who dotes, yet doubts, suspects, yet strongly loves!   170

Oth. O misery!

Iago. Poor and content is rich, and rich enough;
But riches fineless is as poor as winter
To him that ever fears he shall be poor:
Good heaven, the souls of all my tribe defend
From jealousy!

Oth.   Why, why is this!
Think'st thou I'ld make a life of jealousy,
To follow still the changes of the moon
With fresh suspicions? No; to be once in doubt
Is once to be resolved: exchange me for a goat,   180
When I shall turn the business of my soul
To such exsufflicate and blown surmises,
Matching thy inference. 'Tis not to make me
        jealous
To say my wife is fair, feeds well, loves company,
Is free of speech, sings, plays and dances well;

Where virtue is, these are more virtuous:
Nor from mine own weak merits will I draw
The smallest fear or doubt of her revolt;
For she had eyes, and chose me. No, Iago;
I'll see before I doubt; when I doubt, prove;   190
And on the proof, there is no more but this,
Away at once with love or jealousy!

Iago. I am glad of it; for now I shall have reason
To show the love and duty that I bear you
With franker spirit: therefore, as I am bound,
Receive it from me. I speak not yet of proof.
Look to your wife: observe her well with Cassio;
Wear your eye thus, not jealous nor secure:
I would not have your free and noble nature
Out of self-bounty be abused; look to 't: 200
I know our country disposition well;
In Venice they do let heaven see the pranks
They dare not show their husbands; their best
        conscience
Is not to leave 't undone, but keep 't unknown.

Oth. Dost thou say so?

Iago. She did deceive her father, marrying you;
And when she seem'd to shake and fear your
        looks,
She loved them most.

Oth.   And so she did.

Iago.   Why, go to then,
She that so young could give out such a seeming,
To seel her father's eyes up close as oak—   210
He thought 'twas witchcraft—but I am much
        to blame;
I humbly do beseech you of your pardon
For too much loving you.

Oth.   I am bound to thee for ever.

Iago. I see this hath a little dash'd your spirits.

Oth. Not a jot, not a jot.

Iago.   I' faith, I fear it has.
I hope you will consider what is spoke
Comes from my love; but I do see you're moved;
I am to pray you not to strain my speech
To grosser issues nor to larger reach
Than to suspicion.   220

Oth.   I will not.

Iago.   Should you do so, my lord,
My speech should fall into such vile success
As my thoughts aim not at. Cassio's my worthy
               friend—
My lord, I see you're moved.

Oth.   No, not much moved:
I do not think but Desdemona's honest.

Iago. Long live she so! and long live you to think so!

Oth. And yet, how nature erring from itself—

Iago. Ay, there's the point: as—to be bold with you—
Not to affect many proposed matches
Of her own clime, complexion and degree,   230
Whereto we see in all things nature tends—
Foh! one may smell in such a will most rank,
Foul disproportion, thoughts unnatural.
But pardon me: I do not in position
Distinctly speak of her; though I may fear
Her will, recoiling to her better judgement,
May fall to match you with her country forms,
And happily repent.

Oth.   Farewell, farewell:
If more thou dost perceive, let me know more;
Set on thy wife to observe: leave me, Iago.   240

Iago. [*Going*] My lord, I take my leave.

Oth. Why did I marry? This honest creature doubtless
Sees and knows more, much more, than he
               unfolds.

Iago. [*Returning*] My lord, I would I might entreat

          your honour
To scan this thing no further; leave it to time:
Though it be fit that Cassio have his place,
For sure he fills it up with great ability,
Yet, if you please to hold him off awhile,
You shall by that perceive him and his means:
Note if your lady strain his entertainment   250
With any strong or vehement importunity;
Much will be seen in that. In the mean time,
Let me be thought too busy in my fears—
As worthy cause I have to fear I am—
And hold her free, I do beseech your honour.

Oth.   Fear not my government.

Iago.   I once more take my leave.   *[Exit.*

Oth.   This fellow's of exceeding honesty,
And knows all qualities, with a learned spirit,
Of human dealings. If I do prove her haggard,   260
Though that her jesses were my dear
           heart-strings,
I'ld whistle her off and let her down the wind
To prey at fortune. Haply, for I am black
And have not those soft parts of conversation
That chamberers have, or for I am declined
Into the vale of years,—yet that's not much—
She's gone; I am abused, and my relief
Must be to loathe her. O curse of marriage,
That we can call these delicate creatures ours,
And not their appetites! I had rather be a toad,   270
And live upon the vapour of a dungeon,
Than keep a corner in the thing I love
For others' uses. Yet, 'tis the plague of great ones;
Prerogatived are they less than the base;
'Tis destiny unshunnable, like death:
Even then this forked plague is fated to us
When we do quicken. Desdemona comes:

Re-enter Desdemona and Emilia.

    If she be false, O, then heaven mocks itself!
I'll not believe 't.

Des.　　　　　How now, my dear Othello!
Your dinner, and the generous islanders　　　　　280
By you invited, do attend your presence.

Oth.　I am to blame.

Des.　　　　　Why do you speak so faintly?
Are you not well?

Oth.　I have a pain upon my forehead here.

Des.　Faith, that's with watching; 'twill away again:
Let me but bind it hard, within this hour
It will be well.

Oth.　　　　　Your napkin is too little;
　　[*He puts the handkerchief from him; and she drops it.*
Let it alone. Come, I'll go in with you.

Des.　I am very sorry that you are not well.
　　　　　　　　[*Exeunt Othello and Desdemona.*

Emil.　I am glad I have found this napkin:　　　　　290
This was her first remembrance from the Moor:
My wayward husband hath a hundred times
Woo'd me to steal it; but she so loves the token,
For he conjured her she should ever keep it,
That she reserves it evermore about her
To kiss and talk to. I'll have the work ta'en out,
And give 't Iago: what he will do with it
Heaven knows, not I;
I nothing but to please his fantasy.

Re-enter Iago.

Iago.　How now! what do you here alone?　　　　　300

Emil.　Do not you chide; I have a thing for you.

Iago.　A thing for me? it is a common thing—

Emil.　Ha!

Iago.　To have a foolish wife.

Emil.　O, is that all? What will you give me now
For that same handkerchief?

Iago.   What handkerchief?

Emil.   What handkerchief!
          Why, that the Moor first gave to Desdemona;
          That which so often you did bid me steal.

Iago.   Hast stol'n it from her?   310

Emil.   No, faith; she let it drop by negligence,
          And, to the advantage, I being here took 't up.
          Look, here it is.

Iago.   A good wench; give it me.

Emil.   What will you do with 't, that you have been so
                          earnest
          To have me filch it?

Iago.   [*Snatching it*] Why, what's that to you?

Emil.   If 't be not for some purpose of import,
          Give 't me again: poor lady, she'll run mad
          When she shall lack it.

Iago.   Be not acknown on 't; I have use for it.
          Go, leave me.   [*Exit Emilia.*   320
          I will in Cassio's lodging lose this napkin,
          And let him find it. Trifles light as air
          Are to the jealous confirmations strong
          As proofs of holy writ: this may do something.
          The Moor already changes with my poison:
          Dangerous conceits are in their natures poisons,
          Which at the first are scarce found to distaste,
          But with a little act upon the blood
          Burn like the mines of sulphur. I did say so:
          Look, where he comes!

Re-enter Othello.

                          Not poppy, nor mandragora,   330
          Nor all the drowsy syrups of the world,
          Shall ever medicine thee to that sweet sleep
          Which thou owedst yesterday.

Oth.   Ha! ha! false to me?

Iago. Why, how now, general! no more of that.

Oth. Avaunt! be gone! thou hast set me on the rack:
I swear 'tis better to be much abused
Than but to know 't a little.

Iago.   How now, my lord!

Oth. What sense had I of her stol'n hours of lust?
I saw 't not, thought it not, it harm'd not me:
I slept the next night well, was free and merry;   340
I found not Cassio's kisses on her lips:
He that is robb'd, not wanting what is stol'n,
Let him not know 't and he's not robb'd at all.

Iago. I am sorry to hear this.

Oth. I had been happy, if the general camp,
Pioners and all, had tasted her sweet body,
So I had nothing known. O, now for ever
Farewell the tranquil mind! farewell content!
Farewell the plumed troop and the big wars
That make ambition virtue! O, farewell,   350
Farewell the neighing steed and the shrill trump,
The spirit-stirring drum, the ear-piercing fife,
The royal banner and all quality,
Pride, pomp and circumstance of glorious war!
And, O you mortal engines, whose rude throats
The immortal Jove's dread clamours counterfeit,
Farewell! Othello's occupation's gone!

Iago. Is 't possible, my lord?

Oth. Villain, be sure thou prove my love a whore;
Be sure of it; give me the ocular proof;   360
Or, by the worth of man's eternal soul,
Thou hadst been better have been born a dog
Than answer my waked wrath!

Iago.   Is 't come to this?

Oth. Make me to see 't; or at the least so prove it,
That the probation bear no hinge nor loop
To hang a doubt on; or woe upon thy life!

Iago.　My noble lord,—

Oth.　If thou dost slander her and torture me,
　　　Never pray more; abandon all remorse;
　　　On horror's head horrors accumulate;　　　　　　　370
　　　Do deeds to make heaven weep, all earth amazed;
　　　For nothing canst thou to damnation add
　　　Greater than that.

Iago.　　　　　　　O grace! O heaven defend me!
　　　Are you a man? have you a soul or sense?
　　　God be wi' you; take mine office. O wretched
　　　　　fool,
　　　That livest to make thine honesty a vice!
　　　O monstrous world! Take note, take note,
　　　　　O world,
　　　To be direct and honest is not safe.
　　　I thank you for this profit, and from hence
　　　I'll love no friend sith love breeds such offence.　380

Oth.　Nay, stay: thou shouldst be honest.

Iago.　I should be wise; for honesty's a fool,
　　　And loses that it works for.

Oth.　　　　　　　　By the world,
　　　I think my wife be honest, and think she is not;
　　　I think that thou art just, and think thou art not:
　　　I'll have some proof. Her name, that was as fresh
　　　As Dian's visage, is now begrimed and black
　　　As mine own face. If there be cords, or knives,
　　　Poison, or fire, or suffocating streams,
　　　I'll not endure it. Would I were satisfied!　　　390

Iago.　I see, sir, you are eaten up with passion:
　　　I do repent me that I put it to you.
　　　You would be satisfied?

Oth.　　　　　　　Would! nay, I will.

Iago.　And may: but, how? how satisfied, my lord?
　　　Would you, the supervisor, grossly gape on?
　　　Behold her topp'd?

Oth.   Death and damnation! O!

Iago. It were a tedious difficulty, I think,
          To bring them to that prospect: damn them then,
          If ever mortal eyes do see them bolster
          More than their own! What then? how then?   400
          What shall I say? Where's satisfaction?
          It is impossible you should see this,
          Were they as prime as goats, as hot as monkeys,
          As salt as wolves in pride, and fools as gross
          As ignorance made drunk. But yet, I say,
          If imputation and strong circumstances,
          Which lead directly to the door of truth,
          Will give you satisfaction, you may have 't.

Oth. Give me a living reason she's disloyal.

Iago. I do not like the office: 410
          But sith I am enter'd in this cause so far,
          Prick'd to 't by foolish honesty and love,
          I will go on. I lay with Cassio lately,
          And being troubled with a raging tooth,
          I could not sleep.
          There are a kind of men so loose of soul,
          That in their sleeps will mutter their affairs:
          One of this kind is Cassio:
          In sleep I heard him say 'Sweet Desdemona,
          Let us be wary, let us hide our loves;'   420
          And then, sir, would he gripe and wring my hand,
          Cry 'O sweet creature!' and then kiss me hard,
          As if he pluck'd up kisses by the roots,
          That grew upon my lips: then laid his leg
          Over my thigh, and sigh'd and kiss'd, and then
          Cried 'Cursed fate that gave thee to the Moor!'

Oth. O monstrous! monstrous!

Iago.   Nay, this was but his dream.

Oth. But this denoted a foregone conclusion:
          'Tis a shrewd doubt, though it be but a dream.

Iago. And this may help to thicken other proofs   430
          That do demonstrate thinly.

Oth.   I'll tear her all to pieces.

Iago. Nay, but be wise: yet we see nothing done;
She may be honest yet. Tell me but this;
Have you not sometimes seen a handkerchief
Spotted with strawberries in your wife's hand.

Oth. I gave her such a one; 'twas my first gift.

Iago. I know not that: but such a handkerchief—
I am sure it was your wife's—did I to-day
See Cassio wipe his beard with.

Oth.   If it be that,—

Iago. If it be that, or any that was hers,   440
It speaks against her with the other proofs.

Oth. O, that the slave had forty thousand lives!
One is too poor, too weak for my revenge.
Now do I see 'tis true. Look here, Iago;
All my fond love thus do I blow to heaven:
'Tis gone.
Arise, black vengeance, from thy hollow cell!
Yield up, O love, thy crown and hearted throne
To tyrannous hate! Swell, bosom, with thy fraught,
For 'tis of aspics' tongues!

Iago.   Yet be content.   450

Oth. O, blood, blood, blood!

Iago. Patience, I say; your mind perhaps may change.

Oth. Never, Iago. Like to the Pontic sea,
Whose icy current and compulsive course
Ne'er feels retiring ebb, but keeps due on
To the Propontic and the Hellespont;
Even so my bloody thoughts, with violent pace,
Shall ne'er look back, ne'er ebb to humble love,
Till that a capable and wide revenge
Swallow them up. Now, by yond marble heaven,   460
In the due reverence of a sacred vow   [*Kneels.*
I here engage my words.

Iago.   Do not rise yet.   [*Kneels.*

Witness, you ever-burning lights above,
You elements that clip us round about,
Witness that here Iago doth give up
The execution of his wit, hands, heart,
To wrong'd Othello's service! Let him
      command,
And to obey shall be in me remorse,
What bloody business ever.   *[They rise.*

Oth.   I greet thy love,
Not with vain thanks, but with acceptance
      bounteous,   470
And will upon the instant put thee to 't:
Within these three days let me hear thee say
That Cassio's not alive.

Iago. My friend is dead; 'tis done at your request:
But let her live.

Oth.   Damn her, lewd minx! O, damn her!
Come, go with me apart; I will withdraw,
To furnish me with some swift means of death
For the fair devil. Now art thou my lieutenant.

Iago. I am your own for ever.   *[Exeunt.*

SCENE IV

Before the castle.

Enter Desdemona, Emilia, and Clown.

Des. Do you know, sirrah, where Lieutenant Cassio
lies?

Clo. I dare not say he lies any where.

Des. Why, man?

Clo. He's a soldier; and for one to say a soldier lies,

is stabbing.

Des. Go to: where lodges he?

Clo. To tell you where he lodges, is to tell you
where I lie.

·*Des.* Can any thing be made of this?   10

Clo. I know not where he lodges; and for me to
devise a lodging, and say he lies here or he lies
there, were to lie in mine own throat.

Des. Can you inquire him out and be edified by
report?

Clo. I will catechize the world for him; that is,
make questions and by them answer.

Des. Seek him, bid him come hither: tell him I have
moved my lord on his behalf and hope all will
be well.   20

Clo. To do this is within the compass of man's wit,
and therefore I will attempt the doing it.   [*Exit.*

Des. Where should I lose that handkerchief, Emilia?

Emil. I know not, madam.

Des. Believe me, I had rather have lost my purse
Full of crusadoes: and, but my noble Moor
Is true of mind and made of no such baseness
As jealous creatures are, it were enough
To put him to ill thinking.

Emil.   Is he not jealous?

Des. Who, he? I think the sun where he was born   30
Drew all such humours from him.

Emil.   Look, where he comes.

Des. I will not leave him now till Cassio
Be called to him.

Enter Othello.

99

      How is 't with you, my lord?

Oth. Well, my good lady. [*Aside*] O, hardness to
     dissemble!
  How do you, Desdemona?

Des.   Well, my good lord.

Oth. Give me your hand: this hand is moist, my lady.

Des. It yet has felt no age nor known no sorrow.

Oth. This argues fruitfulness and liberal heart:
  Hot, hot, and moist: this hand of yours requires
  A sequester from liberty, fasting and prayer,   40
  Much castigation, exercise devout;
  For here's a young and sweating devil here,
  That commonly rebels. 'Tis a good hand,
  A frank one.

Des.   You may, indeed, say so;
  For 'twas that hand that gave away my heart.

Oth. A liberal hand: the hearts of old gave hands;
  But our new heraldry is hands, not hearts.

Des. I cannot speak of this. Come now, your promise.

Oth. What promise, chuck?

Des. I have sent to bid Cassio come speak with you.   50

Oth. I have a salt and sorry rheum offends me;
  Lend me thy handkerchief.

Des. Here, my lord.

Oth. That which I gave you.

Des. I have it not about me.

Oth. Not?

Des. No, indeed, my lord.

Oth. That's a fault. That handkerchief
  Did an Egyptian to my mother give;
  She was a charmer, and could almost read

The thoughts of people: she told her, while she
        kept it
'Twould make her amiable and subdue my father
Entirely to her love, but if she lost it   60
Or made a gift of it, my father's eye
Should hold her loathed and his spirits should
        hunt
After new fancies: she dying gave it me,
And bid me, when my fate would have me wife,
To give it her. I did so: and take heed on 't;
Make it a darling like your precious eye;
To lose 't or give 't away were such perdition
As nothing else could match.

Des.   Is 't possible?

Oth. 'Tis true: there's magic in a web of it:
A sibyl, that had number'd in the world   70
The sun to course two hundred compasses,
In her prophetic fury sew'd the work;
The worms were hallow'd that did breed the silk;
And it was dyed in mummy which the skilful
Conserved of maidens' hearts.

Des.   Indeed! is 't true?

Oth. Most veritable; therefore look to 't well.

Des. Then would to God that I had never seen 't!

Oth. Ha! wherefore?

Des. Why do you speak so startingly and rash?

Oth. Is 't lost? is 't gone? speak, is it out o' the way?   80

Des. Heaven bless us!

Oth. Say you?

Des. It is not lost; but what an if it were?

Oth. How!

Des. I say, it is not lost.

Oth. Fetch 't, let me see it.

Des. Why, so I can, sir, but I will not now.
This is a trick to put me from my suit:
Pray you, let Cassio be received again.

Oth. Fetch me the handkerchief: my mind misgives.

Des. Come, come;   90
You'll never meet a more sufficient man.

Oth. The handkerchief!

Des.   I pray, talk me of Cassio.

Oth. The handkerchief!

Des.   A man that all his time
Hath founded his good fortunes on your love,
Shared dangers with you,—

Oth. The handkerchief!

Des. In sooth, you are to blame.

Oth. Away!   [*Exit.*

Emil. Is not this man jealous?

Des. I ne'er saw this before.   100
Sure there's some wonder in this handkerchief:
I am most unhappy in the loss of it.

Emil. 'Tis not a year or two shows us a man:
They are all but stomachs and we all but food;
They eat us hungerly, and when they are full
They belch us. Look you, Cassio and my
                    husband.

Enter Cassio and Iago.

Iago. There is no other way; 'tis she must do 't:
And, lo, the happiness! go and importune her.

Des. How now, good Cassio! what's the news with
                    you?

Cas. Madam, my former suit: I do beseech you   110
That by your virtuous means I may again
Exist, and be a member of his love

Whom I with all the office of my heart
Entirely honour: I would not be delay'd.
If my offence be of such mortal kind,
That nor my service past nor present sorrows
Nor purposed merit in futurity
Can ransom me into his love again,
But to know so must be my benefit;
So shall I clothe me in a forced content   120
And shut myself up in some other course
To fortune's alms.

Des.   Alas, thrice-gentle Cassio!
My advocation is not now in tune;
My lord is not my lord, nor should I know him
Were he in favour as in humour alter'd.
So help me every spirit sanctified,
As I have spoken for you all my best
And stood within the blank of his displeasure
For my free speech! You must awhile be patient:
What I can do I will; and more I will   130
Than for myself I dare: let that suffice you.

Iago. Is my lord angry?

Emil.   He went hence but now,
And certainly in strange unquietness.

Iago. Can he be angry? I have seen the cannon,
When it hath blown his ranks into the air,
And, like the devil, from his very arm
Puff'd his own brother; and can he be angry?
Something of moment then: I will go meet him:
There's matter in 't indeed if he be angry.

Des. I prithee, do so.   [*Exit Iago.*
                    Something sure of state   140,
Either from Venice some unhatch'd practice
Made demonstrable here in Cyprus to him,
Hath puddled his clear spirit; and in such cases
Men's natures wrangle with inferior things,
Though great ones are their object. 'Tis even so;
For let our finger ache, and it indues
Our other healthful members even to that sense

Of pain: nay, we must think men are not gods,
Nor of them look for such observancy
As fits the bridal. Beshrew me much, Emilia,   150
I was, unhandsome warrior as I am,
Arraigning his unkindness with my soul;
But now I find I had suborn'd the witness,
And he's indicted falsely.

Emil. Pray heaven it be state-matters, as you think,
And no conception nor no jealous toy
Concerning you.

Des. Alas the day, I never gave him cause!

Emil. But jealous souls will not be answer'd so;
They are not ever jealous for the cause,   160
But jealous for they are jealous: 'tis a monster
Begot upon itself, born on itself.

Des. Heaven keep that monster from Othello's
                mind!

Emil. Lady, amen.

Des. I will go seek him. Cassio, walk hereabout:
If I do find him fit, I'll move your suit,
And seek to effect it to my uttermost.

Cas. I humbly thank your ladyship.
                    [*Exeunt Desdemona and Emilia.*

Enter Bianca.

Bian. Save you, friend Cassio!

Cas. What make you from home?
How is it with you, my most fair Bianca?   170
I' faith, sweet love, I was coming to your house.

Bian. And I was going to your lodging, Cassio.
What, keep a week away? seven days and nights?
Eight score eight hours? and lovers' absent hours,
More tedious than the dial eight score times?
O weary reckoning!

Cas.   Pardon me, Bianca,

I have this while with leaden thoughts been
      press'd;
But I shall in a more continuate time
Strike off this score of absence. Sweet Bianca,
      [*Giving her Desdemona's handkerchief.*
Take me this work out.

Bian.   O Cassio, whence came this?   180
This is some token from a newer friend:
To the felt absence now I feel a cause:
Is 't come to this? Well, well.

Cas.   Go to, woman!
Throw your vile guesses in the devil's teeth,
From whence you have them. You are jealous
      now
That this is from some mistress, some
      remembrance:
No, by my faith, Bianca.

Bian.   Why, whose is it?

Cas. I know not, sweet: I found it in my chamber.
I like the work well: ere it be demanded—
As like enough it will—I'ld have it copied: 190
Take it, and do 't; and leave me for this time.

Bian. Leave you! wherefore?

Cas. I do attend here on the general;
And think it no addition, nor my wish,
To have him see me woman'd.

Bian.   Why, I pray you?

Cas. Not that I love you not.

Bian.   But that you do not love me.
I pray you, bring me on the way a little;
And say if I shall see you soon at night.

Cas. 'Tis but a little way that I can bring you;
For I attend here: but I'll see you soon.   200

Bian. 'Tis very good; I must be circumstanced.

                        [*Exeunt.*

ACT FOURTH
SCENE I

Cyprus. Before the castle.

Enter Othello and Iago.

Iago. Will you think so?

Oth.   Think so, Iago!

Iago.   What,
To kiss in private?

Oth.   An unauthorized kiss.

Iago. Or to be naked with her friend in bed
An hour or more, not meaning any harm?

Oth. Naked in bed, Iago, and not mean harm!
It is hypocrisy against the devil:
They that mean virtuously and yet do so,
The devil their virtue tempts and they tempt
              heaven.

Iago. So they do nothing, 'tis a venial slip:
But if I give my wife a handkerchief—   10

Oth. What then?

Iago. Why, then, 'tis hers, my lord; and being hers,
She may, I think, bestow 't on any man.

Oth. She is protectress of her honour too:
May she give that?

Iago. Her honour is an essence that's not seen;
They have it very oft that have it not:
But for the handerkerchief—

Oth. By heaven, I would most gladly have forgot it:
Thou said'st—O, it comes o'er my memory,   20
As doth the raven o'er the infected house,

Boding to all—he had my handkerchief.

Iago. Ay, what of that?

Oth.   That's not so good now.

Iago.   What,
If I had said I had seen him do you wrong?
Or heard him say—as knaves be such abroad,
Who having, by their own importunate suit,
Or voluntary dotage of some mistress,
Convinced or supplied them, cannot choose
But they must blab—

Oth.   Hath he said anything?

Iago. He hath, my lord; but be you well assured,   30
No more than he'll unswear.

Oth.   What hath he said?

Iago. Faith, that he did—I know not what he did.

Oth. What, what?

Iago. Lie—

Oth.   With her?

Iago.   With her, on her; what you will.

Oth. Lie with her! lie on her!—We say lie on her,
when they belie her.—Lie with her! 'Zounds,
that's fulsome! Handkerchief—confessions—
handkerchief!—To confess, and be hanged for
his labour; first, to be hanged, and then to confess
I tremble at it. Nature would not invest herself   40
in such shadowing passion without some
instruction. It is not words that shakes me thus.
Pish! Noses, ears and lips. Is 't possible?—
Confess?—Handkerchief?—O devil!
                              [*Falls in a trance.*

Iago. Work on,
My medicine, work! Thus credulous fools are
          caught:

And many worthy and chaste dames even thus,
All guiltless, meet reproach. What, ho! my lord!
My lord, I say! Othello!

Enter Cassio.

How now, Cassio!

Cas.   What's the matter?   50

Iago.   My lord is fall'n into an epilepsy:
This is his second fit; he had one yesterday.

Cas.   Rub him about the temples.

Iago.   No, forbear;
The lethargy must have his quiet course:
If not, he foams at mouth, and by and by
Breaks out to savage madness. Look, he stirs:
Do you withdraw yourself a little while,
He will recover straight: when he is gone,
I would on great occasion speak with you.

                                        [*Exit Cassio.*
How is it, general? have you not hurt your head?   60

Oth.   Dost thou mock me?

Iago.   I mock you! no, by heaven.
Would you would bear your fortune like a man!

Oth.   A horned man's a monster and a beast.

Iago.   There's many a beast then in a populous city,
And many a civil monster.

Oth.   Did he confess it?

Iago.   Good sir, be a man;
Think every bearded fellow that's but yoked
May draw with you: there's millions now alive
That nightly lie in those unproper beds
Which they dare swear peculiar: your case is better.   70
O, 'tis the spite of hell, the fiend's arch-mock,
To lip a wanton in a secure couch,
And to suppose her chaste! No, let me know;
And knowing what I am, I know what she shall be.

Oth. O, thou art wise; 'tis certain.

Iago.   Stand you awhile apart;
Confine yourself but in a patient list.
Whilst you were here o'erwhelmed with your grief—
A passion most unsuiting such a man—
Cassio came hither: I shifted him away,
And laid good 'scuse upon your ecstasy;   80
Bade him anon return and here speak with me;
The which he promised. Do but encave yourself,
And mark the fleers, the gibes and notable scorns,
That dwell in every region of his face;
For I will make him tell the tale anew,
Where, how, how oft, how long ago and when
He hath and is again to cope your wife:
I say, but mark his gesture. Marry, patience;
Or I shall say you are all in all in spleen,
And nothing of a man.

Oth.   Dost thou hear, Iago?   90
I will be found most cunning in my patience;
But—dost thou hear?—most bloody.

Iago.   That's not amiss;
But yet keep time in all. Will you withdraw?
                              [*Othello retires.*
Now will I question Cassio of Bianca,
A housewife that by selling her desires
Buys herself bread and clothes: it is a creature
That dotes on Cassio; as 'tis the strumpet's plague
To beguile many and be beguiled by one.
He, when he hears of her, cannot refrain
From the excess of laughter. Here he comes.   100

Re-enter Cassio.

As he shall smile, Othello shall go mad;
And his unbookish jealousy must construe
Poor Cassio's smiles, gestures and light behaviour,
Quite in the wrong. How do you now, lieutenant?

Cas. The worser that you give me the addition
Whose want even kills me.

Iago. Ply Desdemona well, and you are sure on 't.
Now, if this suit lay in Bianca's power,
How quickly should you speed!

Cas.   Alas, poor caitiff!

Oth. Look, how he laughs already!   110

Iago. I never knew a woman love man so.

Cas. Alas, poor rogue! I think, i' faith, she
loves me.

Oth. Now he denies it faintly and laughs it out.

Iago. Do you hear, Cassio?

Oth. Now he importunes him
To tell it o'er: go to; well said, well said.

Iago. She gives it out that you shall marry her:
Do you intend it?

Cas. Ha, ha, ha!   120

Oth. Do you triumph, Roman? do you triumph?

Cas. I marry her! what, a customer! I prithee, bear
some charity to my wit; do not think it so
unwholesome. Ha, ha, ha!

Oth. So, so, so, so: they laugh that win.

Iago. Faith, the cry goes that you shall marry
her.

Cas. Prithee, say true.

Iago. I am a very villain else.

Oth. Have you scored me? Well.   130

Cas. This is the monkey's own giving out: she is
persuaded I will marry her, out of her own love
and flattery, not out of my promise.

Oth. Iago beckons me; now he begins the
story.

Cas. She was here even now: she haunts me in
every place. I was the other day talking on
the sea-bank with certain Venetians; and thither
comes the bauble, and, by this hand, she falls
me thus about my neck— 140

Oth. Crying 'O dear Cassio!' as it were: his gesture
imports it.

Cas. So hangs and lolls and weeps upon me; so
hales and pulls me: ha, ha, ha!

Oth. Now he tells how she plucked him to my
chamber. O, I see that nose of yours, but not
that dog I shall throw it to.

Cas. Well, I must leave her company.

Iago. Before me! look, where she comes.

Cas. 'Tis such another fitchew! marry, a perfumed one. 150

Enter Bianca.

What do you mean by this haunting of me?

Bian. Let the devil and his dam haunt you! What did
you mean by that same handkerchief you gave
me even now! I was a fine fool to take it. I
must take out the work? A likely piece of work,
that you should find it in your chamber, and
not know who left it there! This is some minx's
token, and I must take out the work? There;
give it your hobby-horse: wheresoever you had 160
it, I'll take out no work on 't.

Cas. How now, my sweet Bianca! how now!
how now!

Oth. By heaven, that should be my handkerchief!

Bian. An you'll come to supper to-night, you may;
an you will not, come when you are next
prepared for. [*Exit.*

Iago. After her, after her.

Cas. Faith, I must; she'll rail i' the street   170
else.

Iago. Will you sup there?

Cas. Faith, I intend so.

Iago. Well, I may chance to see you; for I would
very fain speak with you.

Cas. Prithee, come; will you?

Iago. Go to; say no more.   [*Exit Cassio.*

Oth. [*Advancing*] How shall I murder him,
Iago?

Iago. Did you perceive how he laughed at his   180
vice?

Oth. O Iago!

Iago. And did you see the handkerchief?

Oth. Was that mine?

Iago. Yours, by this hand: and to see how he prizes
the foolish woman your wife! she gave it him,
and he hath given it his whore.

Oth. I would have him nine years a-killing. A fine
woman! a fair woman! a sweet woman!

Iago. Nay, you must forget that.   190

Oth. Ay, let her rot, and perish, and be damned
to-night; for she shall not live: no, my heart is
turned to stone; I strike it, and it hurts my
hand. O, the world hath not a sweeter creature:
she might lie by an emperor's side, and
command him tasks.

Iago. Nay, that's not your way.

Oth. Hang her! I do but say what she is: so delicate
with her needle: an admirable musician: O, she

will sing the savageness out of a bear: of so   200
high and plenteous wit and invention:—

Iago. She's the worse for all this.

Oth. O, a thousand thousand times: and then, of so
gentle a condition!

Iago. Ay, too gentle.

Oth. Nay, that's certain: but yet the pity of it, Iago!
O Iago, the pity of it, Iago!

Iago. If you are so fond over her iniquity, give her
patent to offend; for, if it touch not you, it
comes near nobody.   210

Oth. I will chop her into messes: cuckold
me!

Iago. O, 'tis foul in her.

Oth. With mine officer!

Iago. That's fouler.

Oth. Get me some poison, Iago; this night. I'll not
expostulate with her, lest her body and
beauty unprovide my mind again: this night,
Iago.

Iago. Do it not with poison, strangle her in her bed, 220
even the bed she hath contaminated.

Oth. Good, good: the justice of it pleases: very good.

Iago. And for Cassio, let me be his undertaker: you
shall hear more by midnight.

Oth. Excellent good. [*A trumpet within.*] What
trumpet is that same?

Iago. Something from Venice, sure. 'Tis Lodovico
Come from the duke: and, see, your wife is
with him.

Enter Lodovico, Desdemona, and Attendants.

Lod.	God save the worthy general!
Oth.	With all my heart, sir.
Lod.	The duke and senators of Venice greet you. 230
	[*Gives him a letter.*
Oth.	I kiss the instrument of their pleasures.
	[*Opens the letter, and reads.*
Des.	And what's the news, good cousin Lodovico?
Iago.	I am very glad to see you, signior;
	Welcome to Cyprus.
Lod.	I thank you. How does Lieutenant Cassio?
Iago.	Lives, sir.
Des.	Cousin, there's fall'n between him and my lord
	An unkind breach: but you shall make all well.
Oth.	Are you sure of that?
Des.	My lord?
Oth.	[*Reads*] 'This fail you not to do, as you will—' 240
Lod.	He did not call; he's busy in the paper.
	Is there division 'twixt my lord and Cassio?
Des.	A most unhappy one: I would do much
	To atone them, for the love I bear to Cassio.
Oth.	Fire and brimstone!
Des.	My lord?
Oth.	Are you wise?
Des.	What, is he angry?
Lod.	May be the letter moved him;
	For, as I think, they do command him home,
	Deputing Cassio in his government.
Des.	By my troth, I am glad on't.
Oth.	Indeed!

Des.   My lord?

Oth.   I am glad to see you mad.

Des.   Why, sweet Othello?   250

Oth.   Devil!   [*Striking her.*

Des.   I have not deserved this.

Lod.   My Lord, this would not be believed in Venice,
Though I should swear I saw 't: 'tis very much:
Make her amends; she weeps.

Oth.   O devil, devil!
If that the earth could teem with woman's tears,
Each drop she falls would prove a crocodile.
Out of my sight!

Des.   I will not stay to offend you.   [*Going.*

Lod.   Truly, an obedient lady:
I do beseech your lordship, call her back.   260

Oth.   Mistress!

Des.   My Lord?

Oth.   What would you with her, sir?

Lod.   Who, I, my lord?

Oth.   Ay; you did wish that I would make her turn:
Sir, she can turn and turn, and yet go on,
And turn again; and she can weep, sir, weep;
And she's obedient, as you say, obedient,
Very obedient. Proceed you in your tears.
Concerning this, sir,—O well-painted passion!—
I am commanded home. Get you away;
I'll send for you anon. Sir, I obey the mandate,   270
And will return to Venice. Hence, avaunt!
                                   [*Exit Desdemona.*
Cassio shall have my place. And, sir, to-night,
I do entreat that we may sup together:
You are welcome, sir, to Cyprus. Goats and
          monkeys!   [*Exit.*

115

Lod. Is this the noble Moor whom our full senate
Call all in all sufficient? This the nature
Whom passion could not shake? whose solid virtue
The shot of accident nor dart of chance
Could neither graze nor pierce?

Iago.   He is much changed.

Lod. Are his wits safe? is he not light of brain?   280

Iago. He's that he is: I may not breathe my censure
What he might be: if what he might he is not,
I would to heaven he were!

Lod.   What, strike his wife.

Iago. Faith, that was not so well; yet would I knew
That stroke would prove the worst!

Lod.   Is it his use?
Or did the letters work upon his blood,
And new create this fault?

Iago.   Alas, alas!
It is not honesty in me to speak
What I have seen and known. You shall observe him,
And his own courses will denote him so   290
That I may save my speech: do but go after,
And mark how he continues.

Lod. I am sorry that I am deceived in him.   [*Exeunt.*

SCENE II

A room in the castle.

Enter Othello and Emilia

Oth. You have seen nothing, then?

Emil. Nor ever heard, nor ever did suspect.

Oth.   Yes, you have seen Cassio and she together.

Emil.   But then I saw no harm, and then I heard
Each syllable that breath made up between them.

Oth.   What, did they never whisper?

Emil.   Never, my lord.

Oth.   Nor send you out o' the way?

Emil.   Never.

Oth.   To fetch her fan, her gloves, her mask, nor
nothing?

Emil.   Never, my lord.   10

Oth.   That's strange.

Emil.   I durst, my lord, to wager she is honest,
Lay down my soul at stake: if you think other,
Remove your thought; it doth abuse your bosom.
If any wretch have put this in your head,
Let heaven requite it with the serpent's curse!
For if she be not honest, chaste and true,
There's no man happy; the purest of their wives
Is foul as slander.

Oth.   Bid her come hither: go.   [*Exit Emilia.*
She says enough: yet she's a simple bawd   20
That cannot say as much. This is a subtle whore,
A closet lock and key of villanous secrets:
And yet she'll kneel and pray; I have seen her
do 't.

Enter Desdemona with Emilia.

Des.   My lord, what is your will?

Oth.   Pray, chuck, come hither.

Des.   What is your pleasure?

Oth.   Let me see your eyes;
Look in my face.

Des. What horrible fancy's this?

Oth. [*To Emilia*] Some of your function, mistress,
Leave procreants alone and shut the door;
Cough, or cry hem, if any body come:
Your mystery, your mystery: nay, dispatch.   30

[*Exit Emilia.*

Des. Upon my knees, what doth your speech import?
I understand a fury in your words,
But not the words.

Oth. Why, what art thou?

Des. Your wife, my lord; your true and loyal wife.

Oth. Come, swear it, damn thyself;
Lest, being like one of heaven, the devils
themselves
Should fear to seize thee: therefore be double-
damn'd;
Swear thou art honest.

Des. Heaven doth truly know it.

Oth. Heaven truly knows that thou art false as hell.

Des. To whom, my lord? with whom? how am I false?   40

Oth. O Desdemona! Away! away! away!

Des. Alas the heavy day! Why do you weep?
Am I the motive of these tears, my lord?
If haply you my father do suspect
An instrument of this your calling back,
Lay not your blame on me: if you have lost him,
Why, I have lost him too.

Oth. Had it pleased heaven
To try me with affliction; had they rain'd
All kinds of sores and shames on my bare head,
Steep'd me in poverty to the very lips,   50
Given to captivity me and my utmost hopes,
I should have found in some place of my soul
A drop of patience: but, alas, to make me

118

A fixed figure for the time of scorn
To point his slow unmoving finger at!
Yet could I bear that too; well, very well:
But there, where I have garner'd up my heart,
Where either I must live or bear no life,
The fountain from the which my current runs,
Or else dries up; to be discarded thence!   60
Or keep it as a cistern for foul toads
To knot and gender in! Turn thy complexion there,
Patience, thou young and rose-lipp'd cherubin,
Ay, there, look grim as hell!

Des.   I hope my noble lord esteems me honest.

Oth.   O, ay; as summer flies are in the shambles,
That quicken even with blowing. O thou weed,
Who art so lovely fair and smell'st so sweet
That the sense aches at thee, would thou hadst
        ne'er been born!

Des.   Alas, what ignorant sin have I committed?   70

Oth.   Was this fair paper, this most goodly book,
Made to write 'whore' upon? What committed!
Committed! O thou public commoner!
I should make very forges of my cheeks,
That would to cinders burn up modesty,
Did I but speak thy deeds. What committed!
Heaven stops the nose at it, and the moon winks;
The bawdy wind, that kisses all it meets
Is hush'd within the hollow mine of earth,
And will not hear it. What committed!   80
Impudent strumpet!

Des.   By heaven, you do me wrong.

Oth.   Are not you a strumpet?

Des.   No, as I am a Christian:
If to preserve this vessel for my lord
From any other foul unlawful touch
Be not to be a strumpet, I am none.

Oth.   What, not a whore?

Des.   No, as I shall be saved.

Oth.   Is 't possible?

Des.   O, heaven forgive us!

Oth.   I cry you mercy then:
I took you for that cunning whore of Venice
That married with Othello. [*Raising his voice*]
                    You, mistress,   90
That have the office opposite to Saint Peter,
And keep the gate of hell!

Re-enter Emilia.

                              You, you, ay, you!
We have done our course; there's money for
                    your pains:
I pray you, turn the key, and keep our counsel.   [*Exit.*

Emil.   Alas, what does this gentleman conceive?
How do you, madam? how do you, my good lady?

Des.   Faith, half asleep.

Emil.   Good madam, what's the matter with my lord?

Des.   With who?

Emil.   Why, with my lord, madam.   100

Des.   Who is thy lord?

Emil.   He that is yours, sweet lady.

Des.   I have none: do not talk to me, Emilia;
I cannot weep, nor answer have I none
But what should go by water. Prithee, to-night
Lay on my bed my wedding sheets: remember;
And call thy husband hither.

Emil.   Here's a change indeed!   [*Exit.*

Des.   'Tis meet I should be used so, very meet.
How have I been behaved, that he might stick
The small'st opinion on my least misuse?

Re-enter Emilia, with Iago.

Iago. What is your pleasure, madam? How is 't with
      you?   110

Des. I cannot tell. Those that do teach young babes
    Do it with gentle means and easy tasks:
    He might have chid me so; for, in good faith,
    I am a child to chiding.

Iago.   What's the matter, lady?

Emil. Alas, Iago, my lord hath so bewhored her,
    Thrown such despite and heavy terms upon her,
    As true hearts cannot bear.

Des. Am I that name, Iago?

Iago.   What name, fair lady?

Des. Such as she says my lord did say I was.

Emil. He call'd her whore: a beggar in his drink   120
    Could not have laid such terms upon his callet.

Iago. Why did he so?

Des. I do not know: I am sure I am none such.

Iago. Do not weep, do not weep. Alas the day!

Emil. Hath she forsook so many noble matches,
    Her father and her country and her friends,
    To be call'd whore? would it not make one weep?

Des. It is my wretched fortune.

Iago.   Beshrew him for 't!
    How comes this trick upon him?

Des.   Nay, heaven doth know.

Emil. I will be hang'd, if some eternal villain,   130
    Some busy and insinuating rogue,
    Some cogging, cozening slave, to get some office,
    Have not devised this slander; I'll be hang'd else.

Iago. Fie, there is no such man; it is impossible.

Des. If any such there be, heaven pardon him!

Emil. A halter pardon him! and hell gnaw his bones?
    Why should he call her whore? who keeps her
           company?
    What place? what time? what form? what
           likelihood?
    The Moor's abused by some most villanous knave,
    Some base notorious knave, some scurvy fellow.   140
    O heaven, that such companions thou'ldst unfold,
    And put in every honest hand a whip
    To lash the rascals naked through the world
    Even from the east to the west!

Iago.   Speak within door.

Emil. O, fie upon them! Some such squire he was
    That turn'd your wit the seamy side without,
    And made you to suspect me with the Moor.

Iago. You are a fool; go to.

Des.   O good Iago,
    What shall I do to win my lord again?
    Good friend, go to him; for, by this light of heaven,   150
    I know not how I lost him. Here I kneel:
    If e'er my will did trespass 'gainst his love
    Either in discourse of thought or actual deed,
    Or that mine eyes, mine ears, or any sense,
    Delighted them in any other form,
    Or that I do not yet, and ever did,
    And ever will, though he do shake me off
    To beggarly divorcement, love him dearly,
    Comfort foreswear me! Unkindness may do much;
    And his unkindness may defeat my life,   160
    But never taint my love. I cannot say 'whore':
    It doth abhor me now I speak the word;
    To do the act that might the addition earn
    Not the world's mass of vanity could make me.

Iago. I pray you, be content; 'tis but his humour:
    The business of the state does him offence,
    And he does chide with you.

Des. If 'twere no other,—

Iago.   'Tis but so, I warrant. [*Trumpets within.*
Hark, how these instruments summon to supper!
The messengers of Venice stay the meat: 170
Go in, and weep not; all things shall be well.
                    [*Exeunt Desdemona and Emilia.*

Enter Roderigo.

How now, Roderigo!

Rod. I do not find that thou dealest justly with
me.

Iago. What in the contrary?

Rod. Every day thou daffest me with some device,
Iago; and rather, as it seems to me now,
keepest from me all conveniency than suppliest
me with the least advantage of hope. I will
indeed no longer endure it; nor am I yet   180
persuaded to put up in peace what already
I have foolishly suffered.

Iago. Will you hear me, Roderigo?

Rod. Faith, I have heard too much; for your words
and performances are no kin together.

Iago. You charge me most unjustly.

Rod. With nought but truth. I have wasted myself
out of my means. The jewels you have had
from me to deliver to Desdemona would half
have corrupted a votarist: you have told me she   190
hath received them and returned me expectations
and comforts of sudden respect and acquaintance;
but I find none.

Iago. Well; go to; very well.

Rod. Very well! go to! I cannot go to, man; nor 'tis
not very well: by this hand, I say 'tis very
scurvy, and begin to find myself fopped in it.

Iago. Very well.

Rod. I tell you 'tis not very well. I will make myself
known to Desdemona: if she will return me   200
my jewels, I will give over my suit and repent
my unlawful solicitation; if not, assure yourself
I will seek satisfaction of you.

Iago. You have said now.

Rod. Ay, and said nothing but what I protest
intendment of doing.

Iago. Why, now I see there's mettle in thee; and even
from this instant do build on thee a better
opinion than ever before. Give me thy hand,
Roderigo: thou hast taken against me a most   210
just exception; but yet, I protest, I have dealt
most directly in thy affair.

Rod. It hath not appeared.

Iago. I grant indeed it hath not appeared, and your
suspicion is not without wit and judgement.
But, Roderigo, if thou hast that in thee indeed,
which I have greater reason to believe now
than ever, I mean purpose, courage and valour,
this night show it: if thou the next night
following enjoy not Desdemona, take me from   220
this world with treachery and devise engines
for my life.

Rod. Well, what is it? is it within reason and
compass?

Iago. Sir, there is especial commission come from
Venice to depute Cassio in Othello's place.

Rod. Is that true? why then Othello and Desdemona
return again to Venice.

Iago. O, no; he goes into Mauritania, and takes away
with him the fair Desdemona, unless his abode   230
be lingered here by some accident: wherein
none can be so determinate as the removing

of Cassio.

Rod. How do you mean, removing of him?

Iago. Why, by making him uncapable of Othello's
place; knocking out his brains.

Rod. And that you would have me to do?

Iago. Ay, if you dare do yourself a profit and a right.
He sups to-night with a harlotry, and thither will
I go to him: he knows not yet of his honourable   240
fortune. If you will watch his going thence,
which I will fashion to fall out between twelve
and one, you may take him at your pleasure:
I will be near to second your attempt, and he
shall fall between us. Come, stand not amazed
at it, but go along with me; I will show you
such a necessity in his death that you shall
think yourself bound to put it on him. It is now
high supper-time, and the night grows to waste:
about it.   250

Rod. I will hear further reason for this.

Iago. And you shall be satisfied.   *[Exeunt.*

SCENE III

Another room in the castle.

*Enter Othello, Lodovico, Desdemona, Emilia, and
Attendants.*

Lod. I do beseech you, sir, trouble yourself no further.

Oth. O, pardon me; 'twill do me good to walk.

Lod. Madam, good night; I humbly thank your ladyship.

Des. Your honour is most welcome.

125

Oth.   Will you walk, sir?
O,—Desdemona,—

Des. My lord?

Oth. Get you to bed on the instant; I will be returned
forthwith: dismiss your attendant there: look it
be done.

Des. I will, my lord.   10
                [*Exeunt Othello, Lodovico, and Attendants.*

Emil. How goes it now? he looks gentler than he did.

Des. He says he will return incontinent:
He hath commanded me to go to bed,
And bade me to dismiss you.

Emil.   Dismiss me!

Des. It was his bidding; therefore, good Emilia,
Give me my nightly wearing, and adieu:
We must not now displease him.

Emil. I would you had never seen him!

Des. So would not I: my love doth so approve him,
That even his stubbornness, his checks, his
                frowns,—   20
Prithee, unpin me,—have grace and favour in
                them.

Emil. I have laid those sheets you bade me on the bed.

Des. All's one. Good faith, how foolish are our minds!
If I do die before thee, prithee, shroud me
In one of those same sheets.

Emil.   Come, come, you talk.

Des. My mother had a maid call'd Barbara:
She was in love; and he she loved proved mad
And did forsake her: she had a song of 'willow';
An old thing 'twas, but it express'd her fortune,
And she died singing it: that song to-night   30
Will not go from my mind; I have much to do

But to go hang my head all at one side
And sing it like poor Barbara. Prithee, dispatch.

Emil. Shall I go fetch your night-gown?

Des.   No, unpin me here.
This Lodovico is a proper man.

Emil. A very handsome man.

Des. He speaks well.

Emil. I know a lady in Venice would have walked
barefoot to Palestine for a touch of his nether
lip.   40

Des. [*Singing*] The poor soul sat sighing by a
                    sycamore tree,
           Sing all a green willow;
        Her hand on her bosom, her head on her knee,
           Sing willow, willow, willow:
        The fresh streams ran by her, and murmur'd
                    her moans;
           Sing willow, willow, willow;
        Her salt tears fell from her, and soften'd the stones;—
Lay by these:—
[*Singing*] Sing willow, willow, willow;
Prithee, hie thee; he'll come anon:—   50
[*Singing*] Sing all a green willow must be my
                    garland.
           Let nobody blame him; his scorn I approve,—
Nay, that's not next. Hark! who is 't that knocks?

Emil. It's the wind.

Des. [*Singing*] I call'd my love false love; but what
                    said he then?
           Sing willow, willow, willow:
        If I court moe women, you'll couch with moe
                    men.
So get thee gone; good night. Mine eyes do itch;
Doth that bode weeping?

Emil.   'Tis neither here nor there.

Des.   I have heard it said so. O, these men, these men!   60
Dost thou in conscience think,—tell me, Emilia,—
That there be women do abuse their husbands
In such gross kind?

Emil.   There be some such, no question.

Des.   Wouldst thou do such a deed for all the world?

Emil.   Why, would not you?

Des.   No, by this heavenly light!

Emil.   Nor I neither by this heavenly light; I might
do 't as well i' the dark.

Des.   Wouldst thou do such a deed for all the world?

Emil.   The world's a huge thing: it is a great price
For a small vice.

Des.   In troth, I think thou wouldst not.   70

Emil.   In troth, I think I should; and undo 't when I
had done. Marry, I would not do such a thing for
a joint-ring, nor for measures of lawn, nor for
gowns, petticoats, nor caps, nor any petty
exhibition; but, for the whole world,—why, who
would not make her husband a cuckold to make
him a monarch? I should venture purgatory for 't.

Des.   Beshrew me, if I would do such a wrong
For the whole world.

Emil.   Why, the wrong is but a wrong i' the world;   80
and having the world for your labour, 'tis a
wrong in your own world, and you might
quickly make it right.

Des.   I do not think there is any such woman.

Emil.   Yes, a dozen; and as many to the vantage
as would store the world they played for.
But I do think it is their husbands' faults
If wives do fall: say that they slack their duties
And pour our treasures into foreign laps,

Or else break out in peevish jealousies,   90
Throwing restraint upon us, or say they strike us,
Or scant our former having in despite,
Why, we have galls, and though we have some
        grace,
Yet have we some revenge. Let husbands know
Their wives have sense like them: they see and
        smell
And have their palates both for sweet and sour,
As husbands have. What is it that they do
When they change us for others? Is it sport?
I think it is: and doth affection breed it?
I think it doth: is 't frailty that thus errs?   100
It is so too: and have not we affections,
Desires for sport, and frailty, as men have?
Then let them use us well: else let them know,
The ills we do, their ills instruct us so.

Des.   Good night, good night: heaven me such uses
        send,
Not to pick bad from bad, but by bad mend!

                    [Exeunt.

ACT FIFTH
SCENE I

Cyprus. A street.

Enter Iago and Roderigo.

Iago.   Here, stand behind this bulk; straight will he
        come:
Wear thy good rapier bare, and put it home:
Quick, quick; fear nothing; I'll be at thy elbow:
It makes us, or it mars us; think on that,
And fix most firm thy resolution.

Rod.   Be near at hand; I may miscarry in 't.

Iago. Here, at thy hand: be bold, and take thy stand.   [*Retires.*

Rod. I have no great devotion to the deed;
And yet he hath given me satisfying reasons:
'Tis but a man gone. Forth, my sword: he dies.   10

Iago. I have rubb'd this young quat almost to the sense,
And he grows angry. Now, whether he kill Cassio,
Or Cassio him, or each do kill the other,
Every way makes my gain: live Roderigo,
He calls me to a restitution large
Of gold and jewels that I bobb'd from him,
As gifts to Desdemona:
It must not be: if Cassio do remain,
He hath a daily beauty in his life
That makes me ugly; and besides, the Moor   20
May unfold me to him; there stand I in much
    peril:
No, he must die. Be 't so. I hear him coming.

Enter Cassio.

Rod. I know his gait; 'tis he. Villain, thou diest!
                [*Makes a pass at Cassio.*

Cas. That thrust had been mine enemy indeed,
But that my coat is better than thou know'st:
I will make proof of thine.
              [*Draws, and wounds Roderigo.*

Rod.   O, I am slain!
    [*Iago from behind wounds Cassio in the leg, and exit.*

Cas. I am maim'd for ever. Help, ho! murder! murder!   [*Falls.*

Enter Othello.

Oth. The voice of Cassio: Iago keeps his word.

Rod. O, villain that I am!

Oth.   It is even so.

Cas. O, help, ho! light! a surgeon!   30

Oth. 'Tis he. O brave Iago, honest and just,

That hast such noble sense of thy friend's wrong!
Thou teachest me. Minion, your dear lies dead,
And your unblest fate hies: strumpet, I come!
Forth of my heart those charms, thine eyes, are
        blotted:
Thy bed lust-stain'd shall with lust's blood be
        spotted.   *[Exit.*

Enter Lodovico and Gratiano.

Cas.   What, ho! no watch? no passage? murder! murder!

Gra.   'Tis some mischance; the cry is very direful.

Cas.   O, help!

Lod.   Hark!   40

Rod.   O wretched villain!

Lod.   Two or three groan: it is a heavy night:
These may be counterfeits: let's think 't unsafe
To come into the cry without more help.

Rod.   Nobody come? then shall I bleed to death.

Lod.   Hark!

Re-enter Iago, with a light.

Gra.   Here's one comes in his shirt, with light and
        weapons.

Iago.   Who's there? whose noise is this that cries on
        murder?

Lod.   We do not know.

Iago.   Did not you hear a cry?

Cas.   Here, here! for heaven's sake, help me!

Iago.   What's the matter?   50

Gra.   This is Othello's ancient, as I take it.

Lod.   The same indeed; a very valiant fellow.

Iago.   What are you here that cry so grievously?

Cas.   Iago? O, I am spoil'd, undone by villains!
       Give me some help.

Iago.   O me, lieutenant! what villains have done this?

Cas.   I think that one of them is hereabout,
       And cannot make away.

Iago.   O treacherous villains?
       What are you there? come in and give some help.
                     [*To Lodovico and Gratiano.*

Rod.   O, help me here!   60

Cas.   That's one of them.

Iago.   O murderous slave! O villain!
                       [*Stabs Roderigo.*

Rod.   O damn'd Iago! O inhuman dog!

Iago.   Kill men i' the dark! Where be these bloody
                     thieves?
       How silent is this town! Ho! murder! murder!
       What may you be? are you of good or evil?

Lod.   As you shall prove us, praise us.

Iago.   Signior Lodovico?

Lod.   He, sir.

Iago.   I cry you mercy. Here's Cassio hurt by villains.

Gra.   Cassio!   70

Iago.   How is 't, brother?

Cas.   My leg is cut in two.

Iago.   Marry, heaven forbid!
       Light, gentlemen: I'll bind it with my shirt.

Enter Bianca.

Bian.   What is the matter, ho? who is 't that cried?

Iago.   Who is 't that cried!

Bian. O my dear Cassio! my sweet Cassio! O Cassio,
    Cassio, Cassio!

Iago. O notable strumpet! Cassio, may you suspect
    Who they should be that have thus mangled you?

Cas. No.   80

Gra. I am sorry to find you thus: I have been to
        seek you.

Iago. Lend me a garter. So. O, for a chair,
    To bear him easily hence!

Bian. Alas, he faints! O Cassio, Cassio, Cassio!

Iago. Gentlemen all, I do suspect this trash
    To be a party in this injury.
    Patience awhile, good Cassio. Come, come;
    Lend me a light. Know we this face or no?
    Alas, my friend and my dear countryman
    Roderigo? no:—yes, sure: O heaven! Roderigo.   90

Gra. What, of Venice?

Iago. Even he, sir: did you know him?

Gra.   Know him! ay.

Iago. Signior Gratiano? I cry you gentle pardon;
    These bloody accidents must excuse my manners,
    That so neglected you.

Gra.   I am glad to see you.

Iago. How do you, Cassio? O, a chair, a chair?

Gra. Roderigo!

Iago. He, he, 'tis he. [*A chair brought in.*] O, that's
        well said; the chair:
    Some good man bear him carefully from hence;
    I'll fetch the general's surgeon. [*To Bianca*] For
        you, mistress,   100
    Save you your labour. He that lies slain here,
        Cassio,

Was my dear friend: what malice was between you?

Cas. None in the world; nor do I know the man.

Iago. [*To Bian.*] What, look you pale? O, bear him out
            o' the air.
                [*Cassio and Roderigo are borne off.*]
Stay you, good gentlemen. Look you pale, mistress?
Do you perceive the gastness of her eye?
Nay, if you stare, we shall hear more anon.
Behold her well; I pray you, look upon her:
Do you see, gentlemen? nay, guiltiness will speak,
Though tongues were out of use.   110

Enter Emilia.

Emil. 'Las, what's the matter? what's the matter, husband?

Iago. Cassio hath here been set on in the dark
By Roderigo, and fellows that are 'scaped;
He's almost slain, and Roderigo dead.

Emil. Alas, good gentleman! alas, good Cassio!

Iago. This is the fruit of whoring. Prithee, Emilia,
Go know of Cassio where he supp'd to-night.
What, do you shake at that?

Bian. He supp'd at my house; but I therefore shake not.

Iago. O, did he so? I charge you, go with me.   120

Emil. Fie, fie upon thee, strumpet!

Bian. I am no strumpet; but of life as honest
As you that thus abuse me.

Emil.   As I! foh! fie upon thee!

Iago. Kind gentlemen, let's go see poor Cassio dress'd.
Come, mistress, you must tell 's another tale.
Emilia, run you to the citadel,
And tell my lord and lady what hath happ'd!
Will you go on? I pray. [*Aside*] This is the night
That either makes me or fordoes me quite.   [*Exeunt*

SCENE II

A bedchamber in the castle: Desdemona in bed asleep;
a light burning.

Enter Othello.

Oth.   It is the cause, it is the cause, my soul:
Let me not name it to you, you chaste stars!
It is the cause. Yet I'll not shed her blood,
Nor scar that whiter skin of hers than snow
And smooth as monumental alabaster.
Yet she must die, else she'll betray more men.
Put out the light, and then put out the light:
If I quench thee, thou flaming minister,
I can again thy former light restore,
Should I repent me: but once put out thy light,   10
Thou cunning'st pattern of excelling nature,
I know not where is that Promethean heat
That can thy light relume. When I have pluck'd
      the rose,
I cannot give it vital growth again,
It must needs wither; I'll smell it on the tree.
                      [Kissing her.
Ah, balmy breath, that dost almost persuade
Justice to break her sword! One more, one more:
Be thus when thou art dead, and I will kill thee,
And love thee after: one more, and this the last:
So sweet was ne'er so fatal. I must weep,   20
But they are cruel tears: this sorrow's heavenly;
It strikes where it doth love. She wakes.

Des.   Who's there? Othello?

Oth.   Ay, Desdemona.

Des.   Will you come to bed, my lord?

Oth.   Have you pray'd to-night, Desdemona?

Des.   Ay, my lord.

Oth. If you bethink yourself of any crime
Unreconciled as yet to heaven and grace,
Solicit for it straight.

Des. Alas, my lord, what may you mean by that?

Oth. Well, do it, and be brief; I will walk by: 30
I would not kill thy unprepared spirit;
No; heaven forfend! I would not kill thy soul.

Des. Talk you of killing?

Oth.   Ay, I do.

Des. Then heaven have mercy on me!

Oth. Amen, with all my heart!

Des. If you say so, I hope you will not kill me.

Oth.   Hum!

Des. And yet I fear you; for you are fatal then
When your eyes roll so: why I should fear I
              know not,
Since guiltiness I know not; but yet I feel I fear.

Oth. Think on thy sins.

Des.   They are loves I bear to you.   40

Oth. Ay, and for that thou diest.

Des. That death's unnatural that kills for loving.
Alas, why gnaw you so your nether lip?
Some bloody passion shakes your very frame:
These are portents; but yet I hope, I hope,
They do not point on me.

Oth.   Peace, and be still!

Des. I will so. What's the matter?

Oth. That handkerchief which I so loved and gave thee
Thou gavest to Cassio.

Des.   No, by my life and soul!
Send for the man, and ask him.

Oth.   Sweet soul, take heed,   50
Take heed of perjury; thou art on thy death-bed.

Des.   Ay, but not yet to die.

Oth.   Yes, presently:
Therefore confess thee freely of thy sin;
For to deny each article with oath
Cannot remove nor choke the strong conception
That I do groan withal. Thou art to die.

Des.   Then Lord have mercy on me!

Oth.   I say, amen.

Des.   And have you mercy too! I never did
Offend you in my life; never loved Cassio
But with such general warranty of heaven   60
As I might love: I never gave him token.

Oth.   By heaven, I saw my handkerchief in 's hand.
O perjured woman! thou dost stone my heart,
And makest me call what I intend to do
A murder, which I thought a sacrifice:
I saw the handkerchief.

Des.   He found it then;
I never gave it him: send for him hither;
Let him confess a truth.

Oth.   He hath confess'd.

Des.   What, my lord?

Oth.   That he hath used thee.

Des.   How? unlawfully?   70

Oth.   Ay.

Des.   He will not say so.

Oth.   No, his mouth is stopp'd;
Honest Iago hath ta'en order for 't.

Des.   O, my fear interprets! what, is he dead?

137

Oth. Had all his hairs been lives, my great revenge
Had stomach for them all.

Des. Alas, he is betray'd, and I undone!

Oth. Out, strumpet! weep'st thou for him to my face?

Des. O, banish me, my lord, but kill me not!

Oth. Down, strumpet!

Des. Kill me to-morrow; let me live to-night!   80

Oth. Nay, if you strive,—

Des. But half an hour!

Oth.   Being done, there is no pause.

Des. But while I say one prayer!

Oth.   It is too late.   [*He stifles her.*

Emil. [*Within*] My lord, my lord! what, ho! my lord,
          my lord!

Oth. What noise is this? Not dead? not yet quite
                    dead?
I that am cruel am yet merciful;
I would not have thee linger in thy pain:
So, so.

Emil. [*Within*] What, ho! my lord, my lord!

Oth.   Who's there?

Emil. [*Within*] O, good my lord, I would speak a
                    word with you!   90

Oth. Yes: 'tis Emilia. By and by. She's dead
'Tis like she comes to speak of Cassio's death.
The noise was here. Ha! no more moving?
Still as the grave. Shall she come in? were 't
                    good?
I think she stirs again. No. What's best to do?
If she come in, she'll sure speak to my wife:
My wife! my wife! what wife? I have no wife.

O, insupportable! O heavy hour!
Methinks it should be now a huge eclipse
Of sun and moon, and that the affrighted globe   100
Should yawn at alteration.

Emil.   [*Within*] I do beseech you
That I may speak with you, O, good my lord!

Oth.   I had forgot thee: O, come in, Emilia.
Soft; by and by. Let me the curtains draw.
Where art thou?   [*Unlocks the door.*

Enter Emilia.

                    What's the matter with thee now?

Emil.   O, my good lord, yonder's foul murders done!

Oth.   What, now?

Emil.   But now, my lord.

Oth.   It is the very error of the moon;
She comes more nearer earth than she was wont   110
And makes men mad.

Emil.   Cassio, my lord, hath kill'd a young Venetian
Call'd Roderigo.

Oth.   Roderigo kill'd!
And Cassio kill'd!

Emil.   No, Cassio is not kill'd.

Oth.   Not Cassio kill'd! then murder's out of tune,
And sweet revenge grows harsh.

Des.   O, falsely, falsely murder'd!

Emil.   Alas, what cry is that?

Oth.   That! what?

Emil.   Out, and alas! that was my lady's voice.
Help! help, ho! help! O lady, speak again!   120
Sweet Desdemona! O sweet mistress, speak!

Des.   A guiltless death I die.

Emil. O, who hath done this deed?

Des. Nobody; I myself. Farewell:
Commend me to my kind lord: O, farewell!   [*Dies.*

Oth. Why, how should she be murder'd?

Emil.   Alas, who knows?

Oth. You heard her say herself, It was not I.

Emil. She said so: I must needs report the truth.

Oth. She's like a liar gone to burning hell:
'Twas I that kill'd her.

Emil.   O, the more angel she,   130
And you the blacker devil!

Oth. She turn'd to folly, and she was a whore.

Emil. Thou dost belie her, and thou art a devil.

Oth. She was false as water.

Emil.   Thou art rash as fire, to say
That she was false: O, she was heavenly true!

Oth. Cassio did top her; ask thy husband else.
O, I were damn'd beneath all depth in hell,
But that I did proceed upon just grounds
To this extremity. Thy husband knew it all.

Emil. My husband!   140

Oth. Thy husband.

Emil. That she was false to wedlock?

Oth. Ay, with Cassio. Nay, had she been true,
If heaven would make me such another world
Of one entire and perfect chrysolite,
I'ld not have sold her for it.

Emil. My husband!

Oth.   Ay, 'twas he that told me first:
An honest man he is, and hates the slime

140

That sticks on filthy deeds.

Emil.   My husband!

Oth.   What needs this iteration, woman? I say thy
          husband.   150

Emil.   O mistress, villany hath made mocks with love!
         My husband say that she was false!

Oth.   He, woman;
         I say thy husband: dost understand the word?
         My friend, thy husband, honest, honest Iago.

Emil.   If he say so, may his pernicious soul
         Rot half a grain a day! he lies to the heart:
         She was too fond of her most filthy bargain.

Oth.   Ha!

Emil.   Do thy worst:
         This deed of thine is no more worthy heaven   160
         Than thou wast worthy her.

Oth.   Peace, you were best.

Emil.   Thou hast not half that power to do me harm
         As I have to be hurt. O gull! O dolt!
         As ignorant as dirt! thou hast done a deed—
         I care not for thy sword; I'll make thee known,
         Though I lost twenty lives. Help! help, ho! help!
         The Moor hath kill'd my mistress! Murder!
            murder!

Enter Montano, Gratiano, Iago, and others.

Mon.   What is the matter? How now, general!

Emil.   O, are you come, Iago? you have done well,
         That men must lay their murders on your neck.   170

Gra.   What is the matter?

Emil.   Disprove this villain, if thou be'st a man:
         He says thou told'st him that his wife was false:
         I know thou didst not, thou 'rt not such a villain.
         Speak, for my heart is full.

Iago. I told him what I thought, and told no more
Than what he found himself was apt and true.

Emil. But did you ever tell him she was false?

Iago. I did.

Emil. You told a lie, an odious, damned lie;   180
Upon my soul, a lie, a wicked lie!
She false with Cassio! Did you say with Cassio?

Iago. With Cassio, mistress. Go to, charm your tongue.

Emil. I will not charm my tongue; I am bound to speak:
My mistress here lies murder'd in her bed,—

All. O heavens forfend!

Emil. And your reports have set the murder on.

Oth. Nay, stare not, masters: it is true indeed.

Gra. 'Tis a strange truth.

Mon. O monstrous act!

Emil.   Villany, villany, villany!   190
I think upon 't: I think: I smell 't: O villany!
I thought so then: I'll kill myself for grief:
O villany, villany!

Iago. What, are you mad? I charge you, get you home.

Emil. Good gentlemen, let me have leave to speak:
'Tis proper I obey him, but not now.
Perchance, Iago, I will ne'er go home.

Oth. O! O! O!   [*Falling on the bed.*

Emil.   Nay, lay thee down and roar;
For thou hast kill'd the sweetest innocent
That e'er did lift up eye.

Oth.   [*Rising*] O, she was foul!   200
I scarce did know you, uncle: there lies your niece,
Whose breath indeed these hands have newly
                    stopp'd:

142

I know this act shows horrible and grim.

Gra.   Poor Desdemona! I am glad thy father's dead:
Thy match was mortal to him, and pure grief
Shore his old thread in twain: did he live now,
This sight would make him do a desperate turn,
Yea, curse his better angel from his side,
And fall to reprobation.

Oth.   'Tis pitiful; but yet Iago knows   210
That she with Cassio hath the act of shame
A thousand times committed; Cassio confess'd it:
And she did gratify his amorous works
With that recognizance and pledge of love
Which I first gave her; I saw it in his hand:
It was a handkerchief, an antique token
My father gave my mother.

Emil.   O heaven! O heavenly powers!

Iago.   'Zounds! hold your peace.

Emil.   'Twill out, 'twill out. I peace!
No, I will speak as liberal as the north: 220
Let heaven and men and devils, let them all,
All, all, cry shame against me, yet I'll speak.

Iago.   Be wise, and get you home.

Emil.   I will not.

               [*Iago offers to stab Emilia.*

Gra.   Fie!
Your sword upon a woman!

Emil.   O thou dull Moor! that handkerchief thou
            speak'st of
I found by fortune and did give my husband;
For often with a solemn earnestness,
More than indeed belong'd to such a trifle,
He begg'd of me to steal it.

Iago.   Villanous whore!

Emil.   She give it Cassio! no, alas, I found it,   230

And I did give 't my husband.

Iago. Filth, thou liest!

Emil. By heaven, I do not, I do not, gentlemen.
O murderous coxcomb! what should such a fool
Do with so good a wife?

Oth. Are there no stones in heaven
But what serve for the thunder? Precious villain!

> [*He runs at Iago: Iago, from behind,*
> *stabs Emilia, and exit.*

Gra. The woman falls; sure, he hath kill'd his wife.

Emil. Ay, ay: O, lay me by my mistress' side.

Gra. He's gone, but his wife's kill'd.

Mon. 'Tis a notorious villain. Take you this weapon,
Which I have here recover'd from the Moor: 240
Come, guard the door without; let him not pass,
But kill him rather. I'll after that same villain,
For 'tis a damned slave.

> [*Exeunt all but Othello and Emilia.*

Oth. I am not valiant neither,
But every puny whipster gets my sword.
But why should honour outlive honesty?
Let it go all.

Emil. What did thy song bode, lady?
Hark, canst thou hear me? I will play the swan,
And die in music. [*Singing*] Willow, willow,
                     willow.
Moor, she was chaste; she loved thee, cruel Moor;
So come my soul to bliss, as I speak true;   250
So speaking as I think, I die, I die.   [*Dies.*

Oth. I have another weapon in this chamber;
It is a sword of Spain, the ice-brook's temper.—
O, here it is. Uncle, I must come forth.

Gra. [*Within*] If thou attempt it, it will cost thee dear:
Thou hast no weapon, and perforce must suffer.

Oth.   Look in upon me then, and speak with me,
Or, naked as I am, I will assault thee.

Re-enter Gratiano.

Gra.   What is the matter?

Oth.   Behold, I have a weapon;
A better never did itself sustain   260
Upon a soldier's thigh: I have seen the day
That with this little arm and this good sword
I have made my way through more impediments
Than twenty times your stop: but, O vain boast!
Who can control his fate? 'tis not so now.
Be not afraid, though you do see me weapon'd;
Here is my journey's end, here is my butt
And very sea-mark of my utmost sail.
Do you go back dismay'd? 'tis a lost fear:
Man but a rush against Othello's breast,   270
And he retires. Where should Othello go?
Now, how dost thou look now? O ill-starr'd
        wench!
Pale as thy smock! when we shall meet at compt,
This look of thine will hurl my soul from heaven,
And fiends will snatch at it. Cold, cold, my girl!
Even like thy chastity. O cursed slave!
Whip me, ye devils,
From the possession of this heavenly sight!
Blow me about in winds! roast me in sulphur!
Wash me in steep-down gulfs of liquid fire!   280
O Desdemona! Desdemona! dead!
Oh! Oh! Oh!

*Enter Lodovico, Montano, Cassio carried in a chair, and
Officers with Iago, prisoner.*

Lod.   Where is this rash and most unfortunate man?

Oth.   That's he that was Othello: here I am.

Lod.   Where is that viper? bring the villain forth.

Oth.   I look down towards his feet; but that's a fable.
If that thou be'st a devil, I cannot kill thee.

[*Wounds Iago.*

Lod. Wrench his sword from him.

Iago.   I bleed, sir, but not kill'd.

Oth. I am not sorry neither: I'ld have thee live;
For, in my sense, 'tis happiness to die.   290

Lod. O thou Othello, that wert once so good,
Fall'n in the practice of a damned slave,
What shall be said to thee?

Oth.   Why, any thing:
An honourable murderer, if you will;
For nought did I in hate, but all in honour.

Lod. This wretch hath part confess'd his villany:
Did you and he consent in Cassio's death?

Oth. Ay.

Cas. Dear general, I never gave you cause.

Oth. I do believe it, and I ask your pardon.   300
Will you, I pray, demand that demi-devil
Why he hath thus ensnared my soul and body?

Iago. Demand me nothing; what you know, you know:
From this time forth I never will speak word.

Lod. What, not to pray?

Gra.   Torments will ope your lips.

Oth. Well, thou dost best.

Lod. Sir, you shall understand what hath befall'n,
Which, as I think, you know not. Here is a letter
Found in the pocket of the slain Roderigo,
And here another: the one of them imports   310
The death of Cassio to be undertook
By Roderigo.

Oth. O villain!

Cas.   Most heathenish and most gross!

Lod.   Now here's another discontented paper,
Found in his pocket too; and this, it seems,
Roderigo meant to have sent this damned villain;
But that, belike, Iago in the interim
Came in and satisfied him.

Oth.   O the pernicious caitiff!
How came you, Cassio, by that handkerchief
That was my wife's?

Cas.   I found it in my chamber: 320
And he himself confess'd but even now
That there he dropp'd it for a special purpose
Which wrought to his desire.

Oth.   O fool! fool! fool!

Cas.   There is besides in Roderigo's letter,
How he upbraids Iago, that he made him
Brave me upon the watch; whereon it came
That I was cast: and even but now he spake
After long seeming dead, Iago hurt him,
Iago set him on.

Lod.   You must forsake this room, and go with us: 330
Your power and your command is taken off,
And Cassio rules in Cyprus. For this slave,
If there be any cunning cruelty
That can torment him much and hold him long,
It shall be his. You shall close prisoner rest,
Till that the nature of your fault be known
To the Venetian state. Come, bring away.

Oth.   Soft you; a word or two before you go.
I have done the state some service, and they
       know 't.
No more of that. I pray you, in your letters,   340
When you shall these unlucky deeds relate,
Speak of me as I am; nothing extenuate,
Nor set down aught in malice: then must you
       speak
Of one that loved not wisely but too well;
Of one not easily jealous, but, being wrought,

Perplex'd in the extreme; of one whose hand,
Like the base Indian, threw a pearl away
Richer than all his tribe; of one whose subdued
      eyes,
Albeit unused to the melting mood,
Drop tears as fast as the Arabian trees   350
Their medicinal gum. Set you down this;
And say besides, that in Aleppo once,
Where a malignant and a turban'd Turk
Beat a Venetian and traduced the state,
I took by the throat the circumcised dog
And smote him, thus.   *[Stabs himself.*

Lod.   O bloody period!

Gra.   All that's spoke is marr'd.

Oth.   I kiss'd thee ere I kill'd thee: no way but this,
Killing myself, to die upon a kiss.
              [Falls on the bed, and dies.

Cas.   This did I fear, but thought he had no weapon;   360
For he was great of heart.

Lod.   *[To Iago]* O Spartan dog,
More fell than anguish, hunger, or the sea!
Look on the tragic loading of this bed;
This is thy work: the object poisons sight;
Let it be hid. Gratiano, keep the house,
And seize upon the fortunes of the Moor,
For they succeed on you. To you, lord governor,
Remains the censure of this hellish villain,
The time, the place, the torture: O, enforce it!
Myself will straight aboard, and to the state   370
This heavy act with heavy heart relate.   *[Exeunt.*

Glossary

ABHOR, 'it doth a. me,' it is abhorrent to me; IV. ii. 162.

ABOUT, out; I. ii. 46.

ABUSE, deceive; I. iii. 401.

ABUSED, deceived; I. i. 174.

ABUSER, corrupter; I. ii. 78.

ACHIEVED, won; II. i. 61.

ACKNOWN ON 'T, confess any knowledge of it; III. iii. 319.

ACT, action, working; III. iii. 328.

ACTION, accusation; I. iii. 70.

ADDICTION, inclination; II. ii. 6.

ADDITION, honour; III. iv. 194.

ADVANTAGE, 'in the best a.', at the most favourable opportunity;
    I. iii. 298.

ADVISED, careful; I. ii. 55.

ADVOCATION, advocacy; III. iv. 123.

AFFINED, bound by any tie; I. i. 39.

AFFINITY, connexions; III. i. 49.

AGNIZE, confess with pride; I. iii. 232.

AIM, conjecture; I. iii. 6.

ALL IN ALL, wholly, altogether; IV. i. 89.

ALLOWANCE, 'and your a.', and has your permission; I. i. 128.

ALLOWED, acknowledged; I. iii. 224.

ALL'S ONE, very well; IV. iii. 23.

ALMAIN, German; II. iii. 86.

ANCIENT, ensign (F. 1, '*Auntient*'); I. i. 33.

ANTHROPOPHAGI, cannibals (Qq., '*Anthropophagie*'; F. 1,
    '*Antropophague*'); I. iii. 144.

ANTRES, caverns; I. iii. 140.

APART, aside; II. iii. 391.

APPROVE, prove, justify; II. iii. 64.

——, love, adore; IV. iii. 19.

APPROVED, proved to have been involved; II. iii. 211.

APT, natural; II. i. 296.

ARITHMETICIAN, one who has only theoretical knowledge; I. i. 19.

ARRAIGNING, accusing; III. iv. 152.

ARRIVANCE, arrival (Ff., '*Arrivancy*' or '*Arrivancie*'); II. i. 42.
AS, as if; III. iii. 77.
ASPICS, venomous snakes; III. iii. 450.
ASSAY, a test; I. iii. 18.
ASSAY, try; II. i. 121.
ASSURE THEE, be assured; III. iii. 20.
AT, on; I. ii. 42.
ATONE, reconcile; IV. i. 244.
ATTACH, arrest; I. ii. 77.
ATTEND, await; III. iii. 281.

BAUBLE, fool (used contemptuously); IV. i. 139.
BEAR, the Constellation so called; II. i. 14.
BEAR OUT, get the better of; II. i. 19.
BEER, 'small beer,' small accounts, trifles; II. i. 161.
BE-LEE'D, placed on the lee (Q. 1, '*be led*'); I. i. 30.
BESHREW ME, a mild asseveration; III. iv. 150.
BESORT, what is becoming; I. iii. 239.
BEST, 'were b.', had better; I. ii. 30.
BESTOW, place; III. i. 57.
BETIMES, early; I. iii. 383.
BID 'GOOD MORROW', alluding to the custom of friends bidding *good morrow* by serenading a newly married couple on the morning after their marriage; III. i. 2.
BIRDLIME, lime to catch birds; II. i. 127.
BLACK, opposed to 'fair'; III. iii. 263.
BLANK, the white mark in the centre of the butt, the aim; III. iv. 128.
BLAZONING, praising; II. i. 63.
BLOOD, anger, passion; II. iii. 205.
BLOWN, empty, puffed out; III. iii. 182.
BOBB'D, got cunningly; V. i. 16.
BODING, foreboding, ominous; IV. i. 22.
BOND-SLAVES, slaves; I. ii. 99.
BOOTLESS, profitless; I. iii. 209.
BRACE, state of defence; (properly, armour to protect the arm); I. iii. 24.
BRAVE, defy; V. ii. 326.
BRAVERY, bravado, defiance; I. i. 100.
BRING ON THE WAY, accompany; III. iv. 197.
BULK, the projecting part of a shop on which goods were exposed for sale; V. i. 1.

BUTT, goal, limit; V. ii. 267.
BY, 'how you say by', what say you to; I. iii. 17.
——, aside; V. ii. 30.
BY AND BY, presently; II. iii. 309.

CABLE, 'give him c.', give him scope; I. ii. 17.
CAITIFF, thing, wretch; a term of endearment; IV. i. 109.
CALLET, a low woman; IV. ii. 121.
CALM'D, becalmed, kept from motion; I. i. 30.
CANAKIN, little can: II. iii. 71.
CAPABLE, ample; III. iii. 459.
CARACK, large ship, galleon; I. ii. 50.
CAROUSED, drunk; II. iii. 55.
CARVE FOR, indulge (Q. 1, '*carve forth*'); II. iii. 173.
CASE, matter (Ff., '*cause*'); III. iii. 4.
CASHIER'D, sacked; I. i. 48.
CAST, dismissed, degraded from office; V. ii. 327.
CENSURE, judgment; II. iii. 193.
——, opinion, IV. i. 281.
CERTES, certainly; I. i. 16.
CHALLENGE, claim; I. iii. 188.
CHAMBERERS, effeminate men; III. iii. 265.
CHANCES, events; I. iii. 134.
CHARM, make silent, restrain; V. ii. 183.
CHARMER, enchantress, sorceress; III. iv. 57.
CHARMS, magic spells; I. i. 172.
CHERUBIN, cherub; IV. ii. 62.
CHIDDEN, chiding, making an incessant noise; II. i. 12.
CHIDE, quarrel; IV. ii. 167.
CHOLER, anger; II. i. 279.
CHRYSOLITE, a gemstone; V. ii. 145.
CHUCK, a term of endearment; III. iv. 49.
CIRCUMSCRIPTION, restraint; I. ii. 27.
CIRCUMSTANCE, circumlocution; I. i. 13.
——, appurtenances; III. iii. 354.
CIRCUMSTANCED, give way to circumstances; III. iv. 201.
CIVIL, civilized; IV. i. 65.
CLEAN, entirely, altogether; I. iii. 366.
CLIME, country; III. iii. 230.
CLIP, embrace; III. iii. 464.

CLOG, encumber (Ff. 1, 2, 3, *'enclogge'*); II. i. 70.

CLOSE, secret; III. iii. 123.

'CLOSE AS OAK' = 'close as the grain of oak'; III. iii. 210.

CLYSTER-PIPES, tubes used for injection; II. i. 179.

COAT, coat of mail; V. i. 25.

COGGING, deceiving by lying; IV. ii. 132.

COLLIED, blackened, darkened; II. iii. 206.

COLOQUINTIDA, colocynth, or bitter apple; I. iii. 355.

COMMONER, harlot; IV. ii. 72.

COMPANIONS, fellows (used contemptuously); IV. ii. 141.

COMPASSES, annual circuits; III. iv. 71.

COMPLIMENT EXTERN, external show; I. i. 63.

COMPOSITION, consistency; I. iii. 1.

COMPT, reckoning, day of reckoning; V. ii. 273.

CONCEIT, idea; thought (Q. 1, *'counsell'*); III. iii. 115.

CONCEITS, conceives, judges; III. iii. 149.

CONDITION, temper, disposition; II. i. 255.

CONFINE, limit; I. ii. 27.

CONJUNCTIVE, closely united (Q. 1, *'communicatiue'*; Q. 2, *'conjectiue'*);
  I. iii. 375.

CONJURED, charmed by incantations; I. iii. 105.

CONSCIONABLE, conscientious; II. i. 242.

CONSENT IN, plan together; V. ii. 297.

CONSEQUENCE, that which follows or results; II. iii. 64.

CONSERVED, preserved (Q. 1, *'conserues'*; Q. 2, *'concerue'*); III. iv. 75.

CONSULS, senators (Theobald, *'Couns'lers'*; Hanmer, *'counsel'*); I. ii. 43.

CONTENT, joy; II. i. 185.

——, satisfy, reward; III. i. 1.

CONTENT YOU, be satisfied, be easy; I. i. 41.

CONTINUATE, continual, uninterrupted (Q. 1, *'conuenient'*); III. iv. 178.

CONTRIVED, plotted, deliberate; I. ii. 3.

CONVENIENCES, comforts; II. i. 234.

CONVERSE, conversation; III. i. 40.

CONVEYANCE, care; I. iii. 286.

COPE, meet; IV. i. 87.

CORRIGIBLE, corrective; I. iii. 329.

COUNSELLOR, prater (Theobald. *'censurer'*); II. i. 165.

COUNTER-CASTER, accountant (used contemptuously); I. i. 31.

COURSE, proceeding (Q. 1, *'cause'*); II. i. 276.

——, run (Q. 1, *'make'*); III. iv. 71.

COURSER, racehorse; I. i. 113.

COURT AND GUARD OF SAFETY, 'very spot and guarding place of safety' (Theobald, '*court of guard and safety*'); II. iii. 216.

COURT OF GUARD, the main guard-house; II. i. 220.

COURTSHIP, civility, elegance of manners (Q. 1, '*courtesies*'); II. i. 171.

COXCOMB, fool; V. ii. 233.

COZENING, cheating; IV. ii. 132.

CRACK, breach; II. iii. 330.

CREATION, nature; II. i 64.

CRIES ON, cries out (Ff. 2, 3, 4, '*cries out*'); V. i. 48.

CRITICAL, censorious; II. i. 120.

CRUSADOES, Portugese gold coins; so called from the cross on them (worth between six and seven shillings); III. iv. 26.

CRY, pack of hounds; II. iii. 370.

CUDGELLED, beaten; II. iii. 372.

CUNNING, knowledge; III. iii. 49.

CURLED, having hair formed into ringlets, hence affected, foppish; I. ii. 68.

CUSTOMER, harlot; IV. i. 112.

DAFFEST, dost put off (Collier, '*daff'st*'; Qq., '*dofftst*'; F. 1, '*dafts*'); IV. ii. 175.

DANGER, 'hurt to danger', dangerously hurt, wounded; II. iii. 197.

DARLINGS, favourites; I. ii. 68.

DAWS, jack-daws; I. i. 65.

DEAR, deeply felt; I. iii. 260.

DEAREST, most zealous; I. iii. 85.

DEBITOR AND CREDITOR, 'the title of certain ancient treatises on book-keeping; here used as a nick-name' (Clarke); I. i. 31.

DEFEAT, disfigure; I. iii. 346.

——, destroy; IV. ii. 160.

DEFEND, forbid; I. iii. 267.

DELATIONS, accusations; III. iii. 123.

DELIGHTED, delightful; I. iii. 290.

DELIVER, say, relate; II. iii. 219.

DEMAND, ask; V. ii. 301.

DEMERITS, merits; I. ii. 22.

DEMONSTRABLE, 'made d.', demonstrated, revealed; III. iv. 142.

DENOTEMENT, denoting; II. iii. 323.

DEPUTING, substituting; IV. i. 248.

DESIGNMENT, design: II. i. 22.

DESIRED, 'well d.', well loved, a favourite; II. i. 206.

DESPITE, contempt, aversion; IV. ii. 116.

DETERMINATE, decisive; IV. ii. 232.

DEVESTING, divesting; II. iii. 181.

DIABLO, the Devil; II. iii. 161.

DIET, feed; II. i. 303.

DILATE, relate in detail, at length; I. iii. 153.

DIRECTLY, in a direct straightforward way; IV. ii. 212.

DISCONTENTED, full of dissatisfaction; V. ii. 314.

DISCOURSE OF THOUGHT, faculty of thinking, range of thought;
    IV. ii. 153.

DISLIKES, displeases; II. iii. 49.

DISPLEASURE, 'your d.', the disfavour you have incurred; III. i. 45.

DISPORTS, sports, pastimes; I. iii. 272.

DISPOSE, disposition; I. iii. 403.

DISPROPORTION, corruption; III. iii. 233.

DISPROVE, refute; V. ii. 172.

DISPUTED ON, argued, investigated; I. ii. 75.

DISTASTE, be distasteful; III. iii. 327.

DIVISION, arrangement; I. i. 23.

DO, act; I. iii. 395.

DOTAGE, affection for; IV. i. 27.

DOUBLE, of two-fold influence; I. ii. 14.

DOUBLE SET, go twice round; II. iii. 135.

DOUBT, fear; III. iii. 19.

——, suspicion; III. iii. 188.

DREAM, expectation, anticipation; II. iii. 64.

ECSTASY, swoon; IV. i. 80.

EDUCATION, upbringing; I. iii. 182.

ELEMENTS, a pure extract, the quintessence; II. iii. 59.

EMBAY'D, land-locked; II. i. 18.

ENCAVE, hide, conceal; IV. i. 82.

ENCHAFED, chafed, angry; II. i. 17.

ENFETTER'D, bound; II. iii. 351.

ENGAGE, pledge; III. iii. 462.

ENGINES, devices, contrivances, (?) instruments of torture; IV. ii. 221.

ENGLUTS, engulfs, swallows up; I. iii. 57.

ENSHELTER'D, sheltered; II. i. 18.

ENSTEEP'D, steeped, lying concealed under water (Q. 1, 'enscerped');
 II. i. 70.

ENTERTAINMENT, re-engagement in the service; III. iii. 250.

ENWHEEL, encompass, surround; II. i. 87.

EQUINOX, counterpart; II. iii. 129.

ERRING, wandering; III. iii. 227.

ERROR, deviation, irregularity; V. ii. 109.

ESCAPE, escapade, wanton freak; I. iii. 197.

ESSENTIAL, real; II. i. 64.

ESTIMATION, reputation; I. iii. 275.

ETERNAL, damned (used to express abhorrence); IV. ii. 130.

EVER-FIXED, fixed for ever (Qq., 'ever-fired'); II. i. 15.

EXECUTE, to wreak anger; II. iii. 228.

EXECUTION, working; III. iii. 466.

EXERCISE, religious exercise; III. iv. 41.

EXHIBITION, allowance; I. iii. 238.

EXPERT, experienced; II. iii. 82.

EXPERT AND APPROVED ALLOWANCE, acknowledged and proved ability;
 II. i. 49.

EXSUFFLICATE, inflated, unsubstantial (Qq., Ff. 1, 2, 3, 'exufflicate';
 F. 4, 'exufflicated'); III. iii. 182.

EXTERN, external; I. i. 63.

EXTINCTED, extinct; (Ff. 3, 4. 'extinctest'; Rowe, 'extinguish'd');
 II. i. 81.

EXTRAVAGANT, vagrant, wandering; I. i. 137.

FACILE, easy; I. iii. 2.

FALLS, lets fall; IV. i. 257.

FANTASY, fancy; III. iii. 299.

FASHION, conventional custom; II. i. 208.

FAST, faithfully devoted; I. iii. 369.

FATHOM, reach, capacity; I. i. 153.

FAVOUR, countenance, appearance; III. iv. 125.

FEARFUL, full of fear; I. iii. 12.

FELL, cruel; V. ii. 362.

FILCHES, pilfers, steals; III. iii. 159.

FILTH, used contemptuously; V. ii. 231.

FINELESS, without limit, boundless; III. iii. 173.

FITCHEW, pole-cat (used contemptuously); IV. i. 150.

FITS, befits; III. iv. 150.

FLEERS, sneers; IV. i. 83.

FLOOD, sea; I. iii. 135.

FLOOD-GATE, rushing, impetuous; I. iii. 56.

FOLLY, unchastity; V. ii. 132.

FOND, foolish; I. iii. 320.

FOPPED, befooled, duped; IV. ii. 197.

FOR, because (Ff., '*when*'); I. iii. 269.

FORBEAR, spare; I. ii. 10.

FORDOES, destroys; V. i. 129.

FORFEND, forbid; V. ii. 32.

FORGOT, 'are thus f.', have so forgotten yourself; II. iii. 188.

FORMS AND VISAGES, external show, outward appearance; I. i. 50.

FORTH OF, forth from, out of (F. 1, '*For of*'; Ff. 2, 3, 4, '*For off*');
    V. i. 35.

FORTITUDE, strength; I. iii. 222.

FORTUNE, chance, accident; V. ii. 226.

FRAMED, moulded, formed; I. iii. 404.

FRAUGHT, freight, burden; III. iii. 449.

FREE, liberal; I. iii. 266.

——, innocent, free from guilt; III. iii. 255.

FRIGHTS, terrifies; II. iii. 175.

FRIZE, a kind of coarse woollen stuff; II. i. 127.

FROM, contrary to; I. i. 132.

FRUITFUL, generous; II. iii. 347.

FULL, perfect; II. i. 36.

FUNCTION, exercise of the faculties; II. iii. 354.

FUSTIAN, 'discourse f.', talk rubbish; II. iii. 282.

GALLS, rancor, bitterness of mind; IV. iii. 93.

GARB, fashion, manner; II. i. 315.

GARNER'D, treasured; IV. ii. 57.

GASTNESS, fear; V. i. 106.

GENDER, kind, sort; I. iii. 326.

GENEROUS, noble; III. iii. 280.

GENNET, a breed of Spanish horse; I. i. 114.

GIVE AWAY, give up; III. iii. 28.

GOVERNMENT, self-control; III. iii. 256.

GRADATION, order of promotion; I. i. 37.

GRANGE, a solitary farm-house; I. i. 106.

GREEN, raw, inexperienced; II. i. 251.

GRISE, step; I. iii. 200.

GROSS IN SENSE, palpable to reason; I. ii. 72.

GUARDAGE, guardianship; I. ii. 70.

GUARDS, guardians ('alluding to the star Arctophylax', (Johnson); II. i. 15.

GUINEA-HEN, a term of contempt for a woman; I. iii. 317.

GUTTER'D, jagged; II. i. 69.

GYVE, fetter, ensnare; II. i. 171.

HABITS, appearances, outward show; I. iii. 108.

HAGGARD, an untrained wild hawk; III. iii. 260.

HALES, hauls, draws; IV. i. 144.

HAPLY, perhaps; II. i. 280.

HAPP'D, happened, occurred; V. i. 127.

HAPPINESS, good luck; III. iv. 108.

HAPPY, 'in h. time', at the right moment; III. i. 32.

HARD AT HAND, close at hand (Qq., 'hand at hand'); II. i. 268.

HARDNESS, hardship; I. iii. 234.

HASTE-POST-HASTE, very great haste; I. ii. 37.

HAVE WITH YOU, I'll go with you; I. ii. 53.

HAVING, allowance, (?) 'pin-money'; IV. iii. 92.

HEARTED, seated in the heart; III. iii. 448.

HEAVY, 'a h. night', a thick cloudy night; V. i. 42.

——, sad; V. ii. 371.

HEAT, urgency: I. ii. 40.

HELM, helmet; I. iii. 273.

HERSELF, itself: I. iii. 96.

HIE, hasten; IV. iii. 50.

HIGH SUPPERTIME, high time for supper; IV. ii. 249.

HINT, subject, theme; I. iii. 142.

HIP, 'have on the h.', catch at an advantage (a term in wrestling); II. i. 314.

HOLD, make to linger; V. ii. 334.

HOME, to the point; II. i. 166.

HONESTY, becoming; IV. i. 288.

HONEY, sweetheart; II. i. 206.

HOROLOGE, clock; II. iii. 135.

HOUSEWIFE, hussy; IV. i. 95.

HUNGERLY, hungrily; III. iv. 105.

HURT, 'to be h.', to endure being hurt; V. ii. 163.

HYDRA, the fabulous monster with many heads; II. iii. 308.

ICE-BROOK'S TEMPER, i.e. a sword tempered in the frozen brook; alluding to the ancient Spanish custom of hardening steel by plunging red-hot in the rivulet Salo near Bilbilis; V. ii. 252.

IDLE, barren; I. iii. 140.

IDLENESS, unproductiveness, want of cultivation; I. iii. 328.

IMPORT, importance; III. iii. 316.

IMPORTANCY, importance; I. iii. 20.

IN, on; I. i. 137.

INCLINING, favourably disposed; II. iii. 346.

INCONTINENT, immediately; IV. iii. 12.

INCONTINENTLY, immediately; I. iii. 306.

INDEX, introduction, prologue; II. i. 263.

INDIGN, unworthy; I. iii. 274.

INDUES, affects, makes sensitive (Q. 3. '*endures*'; Johnson conj. '*subdues*'); III. iv. 146.

INGENER, inventor (of praises); II. i. 65.

INGRAFT, ingrafted; II. iii. 145.

INHIBITED, prohibited, forbidden; I. ii. 79.

INJOINTED THEM, joined themselves; I. iii. 35.

INJURIES, 'in your i.', while doing injuries; II. i. 112.

INORDINATE, immoderate; II. iii. 311.

INTENDMENT, intention; IV. ii. 205.

INTENTIVELY, with unbroken attention; (F. 1, '*instinctively*'; Ff. 2, 3, 4, '*distinctively*'; Gould conj. '*connectively*'); I. iii. 155.

INVENTION, mental activity; IV. i. 201.

ISSUES, conclusions; III. iii. 219.

ITERATION, repetition; V. ii. 150.

JANUS, the two-headed Roman God; I. ii. 33.

JESSES, straps of leather or silk, with which hawks were tied by the leg for the falconer to hold her by; III. iii. 261.

JOINT-RING, a ring with joints in it, consisting of two halves; a lover's token; IV. iii. 73.

JUMP, agree; I. iii. 5.

——, exactly: II. iii. 392.

JUST, exact; I. iii. 5.

JUSTLY, truly and faithfully; I. iii. 124.

KEEP UP, put up, do not draw; I. ii. 59.
KNAVE, servant; I. i. 45.
KNEE-CROOKING, fawning, obsequious; I. i. 45.
KNOW OF, learn from, find out from; V. i. 117.

LACK, miss; III. iii. 318.
LAW-DAYS, court-days; III. iii. 140.
LEAGUED, connected in friendship (Qq., Ff., *'league'*); II. iii. 218.
LEARN, teach; I. iii. 183.
LEARNED, intelligent; III. iii. 259.
LEETS, days on which courts are held; III. iii. 140.
LEVELS, is in keeping, is suitable; I. iii. 240.
LIBERAL, free, wanton; II. i. 165.
LIES, resides; III. iv. 2.
LIKE, equal; II. i. 16.
LINGERED, prolonged; IV. ii. 231.
LIST, inclination (Ff., Qq. 2, 3, *'leaue'*); II. i. 105.
——, listen to, hear; II. i. 219.
——, boundary; 'patient l.', the bounds of patience; IV. i. 76.
LIVING, real, valid; III. iii. 409.
LOST, groundless, vain; V. ii. 269.
LOWN, lout, stupid, blockhead; II. iii. 95.

MAGNIFICO, a title given to a Venetian grandee; I. ii. 12.
MAIDHOOD, maidenhood; I. i. 173.
MAIN, sea, ocean; II. i. 3.
MAKE AWAY, get away; V. i. 58.
MAKES, does; I. ii. 49.
MAMMERING, hesitating (Ff., Qq. 2, 3, *'mam'ring'*; Q. 1, *'muttering'*
    (Johnson, *'mummering'*); III. iii. 70.
MAN, wield; V. ii. 270.
MANAGE, set on foot; II. iii. 215.
MANDRAGORA, mandrake, a plant supposed to induce sleep;
    III. iii. 330.
MANE, crest; II. i. 13.
MANIFEST, reveal; I. ii. 32.
MARBLE, (?) everlasting; III. iii. 460.
MASS, 'by the mass', an oath (Ff. 1, 2, 3, *'Introth'*; F. 4, *'In troth,'*);
    II. iii. 384.
MASTER, captain; II. i. 211.

MAY, can; V. i. 78.

MAZZARD, head; II. iii. 155.

ME, 'whip me', whip (*me* ethic dative); I. i. 49.

MEAN, means; III. i. 39.

MEET, seemly, becoming; I. i. 146.

MERE, utter, absolute; II. ii. 3.

MINCE, reduce, downplay; II. iii. 247.

MINION, a spoilt darling; V. i. 33.

MISCHANCE, misfortune; V. i. 38.

MIXTURES, intoxicating potions; I. iii. 104.

MOCK, ridicule; I. ii. 69.

MODERN, common-place; I. iii. 109.

MOE, more; IV. iii. 57.

MOLESTATION, disturbance; II. i. 16.

MONSTROUS (trisyllabic) (Capell, '*monsterous*'); II. iii. 217.

MOONS, months; I. iii. 84.

MOORSHIP'S (formed on analogy of worship; Q. 1 reads '*Worship's*');
    I. i. 33.

MORALER, moralizer; II. iii. 301.

MORTAL, deadly; II. i. 72.

——, fatal; V. ii. 205.

MORTISE, 'a hole made in timber to receive the tenon of another piece of
    timber'; II. i. 9.

MOTH, 'an idle eater'; I. iii. 257.

MOTION, impulse, emotion; I. ii. 75, I. iii. 95.

MOUNTEBANKS, quacks; I. iii. 61.

MUMMY, a preparation used for magical,—as well as medicinal,—
    purposes, made originally from mummies; III. iv. 74.

MUTUALITIES, familiarities; II. i. 267.

MYSTERY, trade, craft; IV. ii. 30.

NAKED, unarmed; V. ii. 258.

NAPKIN, handkerchief; III. iii. 287.

NATIVE, natural, real; I. i 62.

NEW, fresh (Qq., '*more*'); I. iii. 205.

NEXT, nearest; I. iii. 205.

NORTH, north wind; V. ii. 220.

NOTORIOUS, notable, egregious; IV. ii. 140.

NUPTIAL, wedding (Qq., '*Nuptialls*'); II. ii. 8.

OBSCURE, abstruse; II. i. 263.

OBSERVANCY, homage; III. iv. 149.

ODD-EVEN, probably the interval between twelve o'clock at night and one o'clock in the morning; I. i. 124.

ODDS, quarrel; II. iii. 185.

OFF, away; V. ii. 331.

OFF-CAPP'D, doffed their caps, saluted (Qq., 'oft capt'); I. i. 10.

OFFENDS, hurts, pains; II. iii. 199.

OFFICE, duty (Q. 1, 'duty'); III. iv. 113.

OFFICED, having a special function; I. iii. 271.

OFFICES, domestic offices, where food and drink were kept; II. ii. 9.

OLD, time-honoured system; I. i. 37.

ON, at; II. iii. 132.

ON 'T, of it; II. i. 30.

OPINION, public opinion, reputation; II. iii. 196.

OPPOSITE, opposed; I. ii. 67.

OTHER, otherwise; IV. ii. 13.

OTTOMITES, Ottomans; I. iii. 33.

OUT-TONGUE, bear down; I. ii. 19.

OVERT, 'o. test', open proofs; I. iii. 107.

OWE, own; I. i. 66.

OWEDST, didst own; III. iii. 333.

PADDLE, play, toy; II. i. 259.

PAGANS, heathen; I. ii. 99.

PAGEANT, show, pretence; I. iii. 18.

PARAGONS, excels, surpasses; II. i. 62.

PARCELS, parts, portions; I. iii. 154.

PARTIALLY, with undue favour (Qq. 'partiality'); II. iii. 218.

PARTS, gifts; III. iii. 264.

PASSAGE, people passing; V. i. 37.

PASSING, surpassingly; I. iii. 160.

PATENT, privilege; IV. i. 209.

PATIENCE (trisyllabic); II. iii. 376.

PECULIAR, personal; III. iii. 79.

PEEVISH, childish, silly; II. iii. 185.

PEGS, 'the pins of an instrument on which the strings are fastened'; II. i. 202.

PERDURABLE, durable, lasting; I. iii. 343.

PERIOD, ending; V. ii. 357.

PESTILENCE, poison; II. iii. 362.

PIERCED, penetrated; I. iii. 219.

PIONERS, pioneers, the commonest soldiers, employed for rough, hard work, such as levelling roads, forming mines, etc.; III. iii. 346.

PITH, strength; I. iii. 83.

PLATFORM, an artillery emplacement; II. iii. 124.

PLEASANCE, pleasure (Qq., *'pleasure'*); II. iii. 293.

PLIANT, convenient; I. iii. 151.

PLUME UP, make to triumph (Q. 1, *'make up'*); I. iii. 398.

POISE, weight; III. iii. 82.

PONTIC SEA, Euxine or Black Sea; III. iii. 453.

PORTANCE, conduct; I, iii. 139.

POSITION, positive assertion; III. iii. 234.

POST-POST-HASTE, very great haste; I. iii. 46.

POTTLE DEEP, to the bottom of the tankard, a measure of two quarts; II. iii. 56.

PRACTICE, plotting; III. iv. 141.

PRATED, talked incessantly; I. ii. 6.

PRECIOUS, used ironically (Qq. 2, 3, *'pernitious'*); V. ii. 235.

PREFER, show, present; I. iii. 109.

——, promote; II. i. 286.

PREFERMENT, promotion; I. i. 36.

PREGNANT, probable; II. i. 239.

PRESENTLY, immediately; III. i. 38.

PRICK'D, incited, spurred; III. iii. 412.

PROBAL, probable, reasonable; II. iii. 344.

PROBATION, proof; III. iii. 365.

PROCREANTS, those who are procreating, having sex; IV. ii. 28.

PROFANE, coarse, irreverent; II. i. 165.

PROFIT, profitable lesson; III. iii. 379.

PROOF, 'made p.', test, make trial; V. i. 26.

PROPER, own; I. iii. 69.

——, handsome; I. iii. 397.

PROPERTY, a person's nature; I. i. 173.

PROPONTIC, the Sea of Marmora; III. iii. 456.

PROPOSE, speak; I. i. 25.

PROPRIETY, 'from her p.', out of herself; II. iii. 176.

PROSPERITY, success; II. i. 288.

PROSPEROUS, propitious; I. iii. 245.

PROVENDER, food; I. i. 48.

PUDDLED, muddled; III. iv. 143.
PURSE, wrinkle, frown; III. iii. 113.
PUT ON, incite, instigate; II. iii. 357.

QUALIFICATION, appeasement; II. i. 282.
QUALIFIED, diluted; II. iii. 41.
QUALITY, 'very q.', i.e. very nature; I. iii. 252.
QUARTER, 'in q.', in peace, friendship; II. iii. 180.
QUAT, pistule, pimple (used contemptuously) (Q. 1, '*gnat*'; Theobald, '*knot*,' etc.); V. i. 11.
QUESTION, trial and decision by force of arms; I. iii. 23.
QUESTS, bodies of searchers; I. ii. 46.
QUICKEN, receive life; III. iii. 277.
QUILLETS, quibbles; III. i. 25.
QUIRKS, shallow conceits; II. i. 63.

RAISED UP, awakened; II. iii. 250.
RANK, coarse; II. i. 315.
——, lustful (? morbid); III. iii. 232.
RECOGNIZANCE, token; V. ii. 214.
RECONCILIATION, restoration to favour; III. iii. 47.
REFERENCE, assignment (Q. 1, '*reuerence*'; Ff. 3, 4, '*reverence*'; Johnson conj. '*preference*'); I. iii. 238.
REGARD, view; II. i. 40.
REGION, part; IV. i. 84.
RELUME, rekindle; V. ii. 13.
REMORSE, pity, compassion; III. iii. 369.
REMOVE, banish; IV. ii. 14.
REPEALS, recalls to favour; II. iii. 363.
REPROBATION, perdition, damnation (Ff., '*Reprobance*'); V. ii. 209.
RESERVES, keeps; III. iii. 295.
RESPECT, notice; IV. ii. 192.
RE-STEM, retrace; I. iii. 37.
REVOLT, inconstancy; III. iii. 188.
RICH, valuable, precious; II. iii. 195.
ROMAN (used ironically); IV. i. 121.
ROUND, straightforward, plain; I. iii. 90.
ROUSE, bumper, full measure; II. iii. 66.
RUDE, harsh; III. iii. 355.
RUFFIAN'D, been boisterous, raged; II. i. 7.

SADLY, sorrowfully; II. i. 32.

SAFE, sound; IV. i. 280.

SAGITTARY, an inn displaying the half-man, half-horse archer sign of Sagittarius; a public building in Venice; I. i. 159.

SALT, lustful; II. i. 245.

SANS, without; I. iii. 64.

'SBLOOD, a corruption of *God's blood*; an oath (the reading of Q. 1; omitted in others); I. i. 4.

SCANT, neglect; I. iii. 268.

SCAPES, escapes; I. iii. 136.

SCATTERING, random; III. iii. 151.

SCION, slip, off-shoot (Qq., '*syen*'; Ff. '*Seyen*'); I. iii. 337.

SCORED ME, 'made my reckoning, settled the term of my life' (Johnson, Schmidt), 'branded me' (Steevens, Clarke); IV. i. 130.

SCORNS, expressions of scorn; IV. i. 83.

SEAMY SIDE WITHOUT, wrong side out; IV. ii. 146.

SECT, cutting, scion; I. iii. 336.

SECURE, free from care; IV. i. 72.

SECURE ME, feel myself secure; I. iii. 10.

SEEL, blind (originally a term in falconry); I. iii. 270.

SEEMING, appearance, exterior; I. iii. 109.

——, hypocrisy; III. iii. 209.

SEGREGATION, dispersion; II. i. 10.

SELF-BOUNTY, 'inherent kindness and benevolence'; III. iii. 200.

SELF-CHARITY, charity to one's self; II. iii. 202.

SE'NNIGHT'S, seven night's, a week's; II. i. 77.

SENSE, feeling (Qq., '*offence*'); II. iii. 268.

——, 'to the s.', i.e. 'to the quick'; V. i. 11.

SEQUENT, successive; I. ii. 41.

SEQUESTER, sequestration; III. iv. 40.

SEQUESTRATION, rupture, divorce; I. iii. 351.

SERVITOR, servant; I. iii. 40.

SHORE, did cut; V. ii. 206.

SHOULD, could; III. iv. 23.

SHREWD, bad, evil; III. iii. 429.

SHRIFT, shriving place, confessional; III. iii. 24.

SHUT UP IN, confine to; III. iv. 121.

SIBYL, prophetess; III. iv. 70.

SIEGE, rank, place; I. ii. 22.

SIMPLENESS, simplicity; I. iii. 247.

SIR, 'play the s.', play the fine gentleman; II. i. 176.

SITH, since (Qq., '*since*'); III. iii. 380.

SKILLET, boiler, kettle; I. iii. 273.

SLIGHT, worthless, frivolous; II. iii. 279.

SLIPPER, slippery; II. i. 246.

SLUBBER, sully, soil; I. iii. 227.

SNIPE, simpleton; (F. 1, '*Snpe*'; F. 2, '*a Swaine*'; Ff. 3, 4, '*a Swain*');
I. iii. 390.

SNORTING, snoring; I. i. 90.

SOFT, mild, gentle; I. iii. 82.

SOFT YOU, hold; V. ii. 338.

SOMETHING, somewhat; II. iii. 199.

SORRY, painful (Qq., '*sullen*'; Collier MS., '*sudden*'); III. iv. 51.

SPAKE, said, affirmed; (Q. 3, '*speake*'); V. ii. 327.

SPARTAN DOG, the dogs of Spartan breed were fiercest; V. ii. 361.

SPEAK I' THE NOSE, 'the Neapolitans have a singularly drawling nasal
twang in the utterance of their dialect; and Shylock tells of "when the
bagpipe sings i' the nose"' (Clarke); (Collier MS., '*squeak*'; *etc.*);
III. i. 5.

SPEAK PARROT, talk nonsense; II. iii. 280.

SPECULATIVE, possessing the power of seeing; I. iii. 271.

SPEND, waste, squander; II. iii. 195.

SPLEEN, choler, anger; IV. i. 89.

SPLINTER, secure by splints; II. iii. 329.

SQUIRE, fellow (used contemptuously); IV. ii. 145.

STAND IN ACT, are in action; I. i. 152.

START, startle, rouse; I. i. 101.

STARTINGLY, abruptly (Ff. 3, 4, '*staringly*'); III. iv. 79.

STAY, are waiting for; IV. ii. 170.

STEAD, benefit, help; I. iii. 344.

STILL, often, now and again; I. iii. 147.

STOMACH, appetite; V. ii. 75.

STOP, 'your s.', the impediment you can place in my way;
V. ii. 264.

STOUP, a vessel for holding liquor; II. iii. 30.

STOW'D, bestowed, placed; I. ii. 62.

STRAIGHT, straightway; I. i. 138.

STRAIN, urge, press; III. iii. 250.

STRANGENESS, estrangement (Qq. '*strangest*'); III. iii. 12.

STUFF O' THE CONSCIENCE, matter of conscience; I. ii. 2.

SUBDUED, made subject; I. iii. 251.

SUCCESS, that which follows, consequence; III. iii. 222.

SUDDEN, quick, hasty; II. i. 279.

SUFFERANCE, damage, loss; II. i. 23.

SUFFICIENCY, ability; I. iii. 224.

SUFFICIENT, able; III. iv. 91.

SUGGEST, tempt; II. iii. 358.

SUPERSUBTLE, excessively crafty (Collier MS., '*super-supple*');
I. iii. 363.

SWEETING, a term of endearment; II. iii. 252.

SWELLING, inflated; II. iii. 57.

SWORD OF SPAIN; Spanish swords were celebrated for their excellence;
V. ii. 253.

TA'EN ORDER, taken measures; V. ii. 72.

TA'EN OUT, copied; III. iii. 296.

TAINTING, disparaging; II. i. 275.

TAKE OUT, copy; III. iv. 180.

TAKE UP AT THE BEST, make the best of; I. iii. 173.

TALK, talk nonsense; IV. iii. 25.

TALK ME, speak to me; III. iv. 92.

TAPER, a light for a candle; I. i. 142.

TELLS O'ER, counts; III. iii. 169.

THEORIC, theory; I. i. 24.

THICK-LIPS, used contemptuously for 'Africans'; I. i. 66.

THIN, slight, easily seen through; I. iii. 108.

THREAD, thread of life; V. ii. 206.

THRICE-DRIVEN, 'referring to the selection of the feathers by *driving* with
a fan, to separate the light from the heavy' (Johnson); I. iii. 232.

THRIVE IN, succeed in gaining; I. iii. 125.

TIME, life; I. i. 162.

TIMOROUS, full of fear; I. i. 75.

TIRE, make tired, weary out; II. i. 65.

TOGED, wearing the toga; I. i. 25.

TOLD, struck, counted (Ff. 3, 4, '*toll'd*'); II. ii. 11.

TOY, fancy; III. iv. 156.

TOYS, trifles; I. iii. 269.

TRASH, worthless thing, dross; II. i. 312.

——, keep back, hold in check (a hunter's term); II. i. 312.

TRAVERSE, march, go on; I. iii. 378.

TRIMM'D IN, dressed in, wearing; I. i. 50. TURN, 't. thy complexion', change colour; IV. ii. 62.
TROTH, truth; IV. i. 249.
TURN, 't. thy complexion', change colour; IV. ii. 62.

UNBLEST, accursed; II. iii. 311.
UNBONNETTED, without taking off the cap, on equal terms; I. ii. 23.
UNBOOKISH, ignorant; IV. i. 102.
UNCAPABLE, incapable; IV. ii. 235.
UNDERTAKER, 'his u.', take charge of him, dispatch him; IV. i. 223.
UNFOLD, reveal, bring to light; IV. ii. 141.
UNFOLDING, communication; I. iii. 245.
UNHANDSOME, unfair; III. iv. 151.
UNHATCH'D, undisclosed; III. iv. 141.
UNHOUSED, homeless, not tied to a household and family; I. ii. 26.
UNLACE, degrade; II. iii. 194.
UNPERFECTNESS, imperfection; II. iii. 298.
UNPROVIDE, make unprepared; IV. i. 218.
UNSURE, uncertain; III. iii. 151.
UNVARNISH'D, plain, unadorned; I. iii. 90.
UNWITTED, deprived of understanding; II. iii. 182.
UPON, incited by, urged by; I. i. 100.
USE, custom; IV. i. 285.
USES, manners, habits (Q. 1. 'vsage'); IV. iii. 105.

VANTAGE, 'to the v.', over and above; IV. iii. 85.
VESSEL, body; IV. ii. 83.
VESTURE, garment; II. i. 64.
VIOLENCE, bold action; I. iii. 250.
VIRTUOUS, having efficacy, powerful; III. iv. 111.
VOICES, votes; I. iii. 261.
VOUCH, assert, maintain; I. iii. 103, 106.
——, bear witness; I. iii. 262.
——, testimony; II. i. 148.

WAGE, venture, attempt; I. iii. 30.
WATCH, watchman; V. i. 37.
WATCH HIM, keep him from sleeping; a term in falconry; III. iii. 23.
WEARING, clothes; IV. iii. 16.

WELL SAID, well done (Qq, '*well sed*'); II. i. 168.

WHAT, who; I. i. 18.

WHEELING, errant (Q. 2, '*wheedling*'); I. i. 137.

WHIPSTER, one who whips out his sword (used contemptuously); V. ii. 244.

WHITE (used with a play upon *white* and *wight*); II. i. 134.

WHOLESOME, reasonable; III. i. 49.

WICKER, covered with wicker-work (Ff. '*Twiggen*'); II. iii. 152.

WIGHT, person (applied to both sexes); II. i. 159.

WIND, 'let her down the w.'; 'the falconers always let the hawk fly against the wind; if she flies with the wind behind her she seldom returns. If therefore a hawk was for any reason to be dismissed, she was *let down the wind*, and from that time shifted for herself and *preyed at fortune*' (Johnson); III. iii. 262.

WIND-SHAKED, wind-shaken; II. i. 13.

WITH, by; II. i. 34.

WITHAL, with; I. iii. 93.

WITH ALL MY HEART, used both as a salutation, and also as a reply to a salutation; IV. i. 229.

WITHIN DOOR, 'speak w. d.', i.e. 'not so loud as to be heard outside the house'; IV. ii. 144.

WOMAN'D, accompanied by a woman; III. iv. 195.

WORSER, worse; I. i. 95.

WRENCH, wrest (Q. 1, '*Wring*'); V. ii. 288.

WRETCH, a term of endearment (Theobald, '*wench*'); III. iii. 90.

WROUGHT, worked upon; V. ii. 345.

YERK'D, thrust; I. ii. 5.

YET, as yet, till now; III. iii. 432.

ZOUNDS, an abbreviated oath meaning 'By God's wounds'; I. i. 86.

Notes

I. i. 2–3. *'who hast had ... strings were thine'* = who has been using my money as if it were their own.

I. i. 9. *'In personal suit'* = Making a direct personal request.

I. i. 13–14. *'Evades them, with ... epithets of war'* = Evades implementing his plans with grandiose declarations replete with military platitudes.

I. i. 15. Omitted in Ff. and Qq. 2, 3.

I. i. 21. *'A fellow almost damn'd in a fair wife'*. This line is much debated. A possible interpretation is that Cassio is totally unsuited to having a decent wife, while some have seen it as meaning that he will always be tempted to sin with another man's wife.

I. i. 30–31. *'must be be-lee'd ... debitor and creditor'* = must have the wind taken out of my sails by a mere bookkeeper.

I. i. 36–38. *'Preferment goes by ... to the first'* = Promotion goes to those with private recommendation and connections and not by the traditions of seniority.

I. i. 49. *'Whip me such honest knaves'* = I do not care for such honest fools.

I. i. 57–58. *'Were I the ... follow but myself'* = If I were Othello I wouldn't be myself, and by following him I serve my own self-interest.

I. i. 62–63. *'The native act ... In compliment extern'* = My internal behaviours and tendencies conform with my outward behaviour.

I. i. 72. *'changes'*; Ff. read *'chances'*.

I. i. 99–101. *'Being full of ... start my quiet'* = As you are full of food and intoxicating drink, you have come to disturb my peace with malicious intent.

I. i. 117–118. *'making the beast with two backs'* = having sex.

I. i. 124. *'At this odd-even ... watch o' the night'* = During these early hours of the morning, when the watch is boring.

I. i. 135. *'hath made a gross revolt'* = has made a disgusting act of rebellion.

I. i. 137–138. *'In an extravagant ... and every where'* = To a wandering and roaming foreigner who goes wherever he wants.

I. i. 146. *'It seems not ... to my place'* = It does not seem acceptable, nor appropriate to my position.

I. i. 149. *'However this may ... with some check'* = However this might bring him a setback.

I. i. 184. *'I'll deserve your pains'* = I'll reward you for your effort.

I. ii. 2. *'very stuff o' the conscience'* = the essential principle.

I. ii. 3–4. *'I lack iniquity ... do me service'* = I lack the sinfulness to advance my career.

I. ii. 13–14. *'And hath in his effect a voice potential ... as the duke's'* = He has at his disposal an authority as powerful as the Duke's.

I. ii. 27. *'Put into circumscription and confine'* = Put him under confinement and into prison.

I. ii. 50. *'he to-night hath boarded a land carack'* = tonight he has boarded and captured a large trading ship (i.e. one with lots of treasure).

I. ii. 64. *'I'll refer me to all things of sense'* = I'll assess matter through common sense.

I. ii. 72–77; iii. 16, 36, 63, 118, 123, 194; omitted Q. 1.

I. ii. 75. *'weaken motion'*; Rowe's emendation; Ff. and Qq. 2, 3, *'weakens motion'*; Pope (Ed. 2, Theobald) *'weaken notion'*; Hammer, *'waken motion'*; Keightley, *'wakens motion'*; Anon. conj. in Furness *'wake emotion'*, &c.

I. ii. 78–79. *'a practiser / Of ... out of warrant'* = a practitioner of dark, forbidden magic.

I. iii. 5–7. *'jump not on ... oft with difference'* = the reports do not agree on exact numbers, and where guesswork is used there are often differences.

I. iii. 11. *'the main article I do approve'* = I approve of the general sense of the report.

I. iii. 19. *'false gaze'* = wrong direction (i.e. the Rhodes fleet is a decoy).

I. iii. 24. *'For that it ... such warlike brace'* = For its defences are not well prepared.

I. iii. 29–30. *'Neglecting an attempt ... a danger profitless'* = Ignoring the chance for an easy win to provoke and risk a danger with little advantage.

I. iii. 64. *'Sans witchcraft could not'* = It could not happen without witchcraft.

I. iii. 67. *'bloody book of law'*; 'By the Venetian law the giving of love-potions was highly criminal' (Clarke).

I. iii. 80–81. *'The very head ... extent, no more'* = My greatest offence is this, no more, no less.

I. iii. 83–85. *'For since these ... the tented field'* = For as my arms have seven years' strength, until some nine months ago, their greatest service has been in military campaigns.

I. iii. 87. *'feats of broil'*; Capell's emendation; Q. 1, *'feate of broile'*; F. 1, *'Feats of Broiles'*, &c.

I. iii. 107. *'Certain'*; so Qq.; Ff., *'wider'*.

I. iii. 111. *'indirect and forced courses'* = devious and coercive measures.

I. iii. 114. *'As soul to soul affordeth'* = By open connection, one person with another.

I. iii. 136. *'Of hair-breadth ... imminent deadly breach'* = Of hair-raising battles in breached walls (of a fortification under attack).

I. iii. 139. *'portance in my'*; so Ff. and Q. 2; Q. 3, *'portence in my'*;

Q. 1, *'with it all my'*; Johnson conj. *'portance in't; my'*; &c.; *'travels"*; the reading of Modern Edd. (Globe Ed.); Qq., *'travells'*; Pope, *'travel's'*; F. 1, *'Trauellours'*; Ff. 2, 3, *'Travellers'*; F. 4, *'Traveller's'*; Richardson conj. *'travellous'* or *'travailous'*.

I. iii. 159. *'sighs'*; Ff., *'kisses'*; Southern MS., *'thanks'*.

I. iii. 173. *'Take up this ... at the best'* = Make the best of this whole confused business.

I. iii. 174–175. *'Men do their ... their bare hands'* = Men will work with what's available rather than resort to their bare hands.

I. iii. 198. *'To hang clogs on them'* = To put them in wooden clamps around their legs.

I. iii. 207. *'Patience her injury a mockery makes'* = Patient endurance robs misfortune of its power.

I. iii. 212–215. *'He bears the ... poor patience borrow'* = A man endures misfortune if he hears comforting words, but if sorrow overwhelms his patience, guilt at his weakness is added to the punishment and the grief.

I. iii. 224–225 *'a substitute of most allowed / sufficiency'* = a deputy of trusted competence.

I. iii. 232–234. 'I do agnize ... find in hardness' = I accept that I have the capacity to respond well to tough situations.

I. iii. 250. *'and storm of fortunes'*; Q. 1, *'and scorne of Fortunes'*, &c.

I. iii. 250–251. *'My downright violence ... to the world'* = The speed and greatness of my decision proclaims the rightness of my actions.

I. iii. 261. *'Let her have your voices'*; Dyce's correction; Ff., *'Let her have your voice'*; Qq. read:—

> *'Your voyces Lords; beseech you let her will*
> *Haue a free way,'*

I. iii. 263. *'the palate of my appetite'* = my sexual desires.

I. iii. 264–265. *'the young affects In me defunct'*; Qq., *'the young affects In my defunct'*; so F. 1; Ff. 2, 3, 4 (*'effects'*). The reading of the text is the simplest and most plausible emendation of the many proposed, the words meaning 'the passions of youth which I have now outlived': *'proper satisfaction'* = 'my own gratification'.

I. iii. 270–272. *'seel with wanton ... taint my business'* = If the fluttering contrivances of Cupid cloud my duty with sensuality and lust, and so affect my work.

I. iii. 330. *'balance'*; Ff., 'brain' and *'braine'*; Theobald, *'beam'*.

I. iii. 350. *'it was a violent commencement'* = her love started suddenly and powerfully.

I. iii. 354–355. *'luscious as locusts'*; 'perhaps so mentioned from being placed together with wild honey in St Matthew iii.4' (Schmidt).

I. iii. 358. Omitted in Ff.

I. iii. 387. The reading in the text is that of the second and third Quartos; Q. 1, adds after the words *'I am chang'd'*: *'Goe to, farewell, put money enough in your purse'*; omitting *'I'll go sell all my land'*.

I. iii. 395–396. *'But I for ... if for surety'* = I will act as if mere suspicion is absolutely true.

I. iii. 399–400. *'plume up my ... In double knavery'* = flatter my ego with skilful deceit.

II. i. 39–40. *'Even till we ... An indistinct regard'* = Until the division between sea and sky is blurred.

II. i. 50. *'not surfeited to death'* = not overcome by fear of death.

II. i. 62. *'That paragons description and wild fame'* = That exceeds the descriptions and praise of her.

II. i. 65. *'tire the ingener'*; Knight, Steevens conj.; F. 1, *'tyre the Ingeniuer'*; Ff. 2, 3, 4, *'tire the Ingeniver'*; Q. 1, *'beare all Excellency'*—; Qq. 2, 3, *'beare an excelency'*:—Johnson conj. *'tire the ingenious verse'*; Pope, *'beare all excellency—'*

II. i. 82. *'And ... Cyprus'*; omitted in Ff.

II. i. 101–103. *'Sir, would she … You'ld have enough.'* = If she kissed you as much as she rebuked me, you would be satisfied.

II. i. 106–108. *'Marry, before your … chides with thinking'* = Certainly, she keeps silent on some matters while scolding me with her thoughts.

II. i. 127. *'Comes from my … does from frize'* = Comes from my imagination like pulling sticky birdlime from woollen cloth.

II. i. 146–148. *'one that in … very malice itself?'* = one who extracted approval even from malicious people.

II. i. 161. *'To suckle fools and chronicle small beer'* = To nurse infants and keep petty accounts.

II. i. 202. *'But I'll set … make this music'* = But I will detune the strings that make this music (and therefore sow discord).

II. i. 208–209. *'I prattle out … mine own comforts'* = I'm uncharacteristically garrulous and talk constantly about my happiness.

II. i. 239–240. *'as it is … and unforced position'* = as it is a most obvious and natural understanding.

II. i. 248. *'stamp and counterfeit advantages'* = create and engineer opportunities.

II. i. 249. *'a devilish knave'*; omitted in Qq.

II. i. 258. *'blest pudding'*; Ff. *'Bless'd pudding'*; omitted in Qq.

II. i. 268–269. *'comes the master and main'*; so Ff.; Q. 1 reads *'comes the maine'*; Qq. 2, 3, *'comes Roderigo, the master and the maine'*.

II. i. 280. *'haply may'*; Qq. read *'haply with his Trunchen may'*.

II. i. 312. *'poor trash of Venice, whom I trash'*; Steevens' emendation; Q. 1, *'poor trash … I crush'*; Ff., Qq. 2, 3, *'poor Trash … I trace'*; Theobald, Warburton conj. *'poor brach … I trace'*; Warburton (later conj.) *'poor brach … I cherish'*.

II. i. 313. *'stand the putting on'* = can rise to my challenge.

II. i. 316. *'For I fear Cassio with my night-cap too'* = I fear that Cassio has had sexual relations with my wife.

II. iii. 9. *'The purchase made, the fruits are to ensue'*. Othello uses a business metaphor as innuendo for permission to have marital sex.

II. iii. 22–23. *'parley / to provocation'* = incitement to lust.

II. iii. 31. *'a brace of Cyprus gallants'* = a pair of Cypriot young men.

II. iii. 42. *'here'*, i.e. in my head.

II. iii. 58. *'That hold their … a wary distance'* = Who quickly turn aggressive if they think their honour has been questioned.

II. iii. 85–86. *'he sweats not to overthrow your / Almain'* = He can outdrink a German without breaking a sweat.

II. iii. 92–99. These lines are from an old song called *'Take thy old cloak about thee'*, to be found in Percy's *Reliques*.

II. iii. 114. *'lieutenant is to ... before the ancient'* = rank takes precedence over more experienced lower ranks.

II. iii. 129–130. *''Tis to his ... as the other'* = Like the balance of daylight on the equinox, vice is equal to his virtue.

II. iii. 174. *'Holds his soul light'* = Does not place value on his life.

II. iii. 167. *'sense of place'*; Hanmer's emendation of Qq., Ff., *'place of sense'*.

II. iii. 186–187. *'And would in ... part of it!'* = I would rather have lost my legs in battle than have been involved in this disgrace.

II. iii. 216. *'on the court and guard of safety'* = within the headquarters that should warrant the island's safety.

II. iii. 220. *'Touch me not so near'* = Don't press me to explain.

II. iii. 273–275. *'you are but ... than in malice'* = You are only temporarily subject to his bad mood, which only expresses the politics of the present (and will therefore pass).

II. iii. 311–312. *'Every inordinate cup ... is a devil'* = Every excessively alcoholic drink is an evil tool of the devil.

II. iii. 318–319. *'some time'*; so Qq.; Ff., *'a time'*; Grant White, *'one time'*.

II. iii. 347–348. *'She's framed as ... the free elements'* = She is as generous as the elements of nature.

II. iii. 350. *'All seals and symbols of redeemed sin'* = All the covenants and signs of Christian faith.

II. iii. 394. *'Dull not device by coldness and delay'* = Don't lose momentum through apathy or procrastination.

III. i. 4. *'speak i' the nose thus'* = make a nasal sound. From the way that the Neapolitan accent was meant to sound nasal; also associated with the effect on the nose of syphilis, a disease reputed to have begun in Naples.

III. i. 13. *'for love's sake'*; Q. 1, *'of all loues'*.

III. i. 43. *'Florentine'*, i.e. 'even a Florentine'; Iago was a Venetian.

III. i. 51–53. *'And needs no ... you in again'* = He doesn't need anyone else to intercede to bring you back into his favour.

III. iii. 16. *'Or breed itself so out of circumstance'* = Eventually outgrow the original situation.

III. iii. 23. *'I'll watch him ... out of patience'* = I'll tame him by keeping him awake and talking to him until he gives in.

III. iii. 65–67. *'Save that, they ... a private check'* = Except that in wartime examples are made of the very best men – the crime is small enough to warrant just a private reprimand.

III. iii. 82. *'poise and difficult weight'* = substantial and significant importance.

III. iii. 106. *'By heaven, he echoes me'*; Q. 1, *'By heauen he ecchoes me'*; Ff., *'Alas, thou ecchos't me'*; Qq. 2, 3, *'why dost thou ecchoe me.'*

III. iii. 123–124. *'They're close delations ... passion cannot rule'* = They are secret thoughts that are so powerful emotion cannot control them.

III. iii. 127. *'would they might seem none!'* = then I wish that they would seem to be not what they are.

III. iii. 132. *'thy worst of thoughts'*; so Ff., Q. 2; Q. 1, reads *'the worst of thoughts'*; Q. 3, *'thy thoughts'*; perhaps we should read: *'As thou dost rum'nate, give thy worst of thoughts.'*

III. iii. 135. *'I am not ... are free to'* = that which even slaves are not bound to.

III. iii. 146–147. *'it is my ... spy into abuses'* = it is a fault of my character to investigate transgressions.

III. iii. 160–161. *'Robs me of... me poor indeed'* = Takes from me something that is worthless to him, even though it bankrupts me.

III. iii. 166–167. *'It is the ... it feeds on'* = Jealousy feeds on the person who has it and makes him look ever more ridiculous.

III. iii. 170. *'strongly'*; so Qq.; Ff., *'soundly'*; Knight, *'fondly'*.

III. iii. 179–180. *'to be once ... be resolved'* = as soon as I suspect something is wrong then I have to act.

III. iii. 218–220. *'I am to ... Than to suspicion'* = I implore you not to take what I say and expand it to more outrageous conclusions, and go beyond mere suspicion.

III. iii. 229–230. *'Not to affect ... complexion and degree'* = Rejecting many marriage proposals from those of her own country, ethnicity and status.

III. iii. 237–238. *'May fall to ... And happily repent'* = She might start unfavourably to compare your appearance to that of her countrymen.

III. iii. 253. *'Let me be ... in my fears'* = Regard my worrying as excessive.

III. iii. 274–275. *'Prerogatived are they ... unshunnable, like death'* = Great figures have fewer rights than those at the bottom of society, as they have less chance of faithful wives – it is an inevitable fate, like death.

III. iii. 277. *'Desdemona comes'*; so Qq.; Ff. read *'Looke where she comes.'*

III. iii. 322–324. *'Trifles light as ... of holy writ:'* = To jealous people insignificant things can seem like proof with the infallibility of holy scripture.

III. iii. 325, 383–390, 453–460; iv. 8–10, 195–196. Omitted in Q. 1.

III. iii. 335. *'thou hast set me on the rack'* = you are torturing me (as if on the rack).

III. iii. 355–356. *'O you mortal ... dread clamours counterfeit'* = O heavy siege weapons, whose thunder in battle imitates the thunderbolts of Jove.

III. iii. 388–390. *'If there be ... not endure it.'* = I will not endure this agony if there are nooses, knives, poison, fire or drowning rivers to hand.

III. iii. 440. *'any that was hers'*; Malone's emendation; Qq., *'any, it was hers'*; F. 1, *'any, it was hers'*; Ff. 2, 3, 4, *'any, if 't was hers'*; Anon conj. *'any "it" was hers'*.

III. iii. 447. *'thy hollow cell'*; so Qq.; Ff. read *'the hollow hell'*; Warburton, *'th' unhallow'd cell'*.

III. iii. 449–450. *'Swell, bosom, with ... aspics' tongues!'* = My bosom is heaving as if full of poisonous snakes.

III. iii. 456. Steevens compares the following passage in Holland's *Pliny*:— 'And the sea Pontus ever more floweth and runneth out from Propontes, but the sea never retireth back again within Pontus.'

III. iii. 469. *'business ever'*; Qq., *'worke so euer'*; Collier, *'work soe'er'*; &c.

III. iv. 8–9. *'To tell you ... where I lie'* = I would be lying if I told you where he stays.

III. iv. 16. *'I will catechize the world'* = I will interrogate everyone.

III. iv. 46–47. *'the hearts of ... hands, not hearts'* = People in the past gave their hearts to each other, now they just give their hands.

III. iv. 65. *'her'*, i.e. to my wife (implied in *'wive'*).

III. iv. 103. *''Tis not a ... us a man'* = It takes one or two years for a man to reveal his true character.

III. iv. 120–122. *'So shall I ... To fortune's alms'* = So I shall pursue a different type of life and surrender my direction to fortune.

III. iv. 134–137. *'I have seen ... he be angry?'* = I have seen cannon blast his troops into the air, and with the devil's power destroy the comrade next to him, so his anger must be great.

III. iv. 151. *'warrior'*; Hanmer *'wrangler'*; cp. *'O my fair warrior'* (II. i. 184).

III. iv. 174–175. *'and lovers' absent ... eight score times?'* = for lovers, the time spent separated seems far longer than the time on the clock.

III. iv. 177. *'leaden thoughts been press'd'* = weighed down by heavy thoughts.

IV. i. 6–8. *'It is hypocrisy ... they tempt heaven'* = It is hypocritical to the devil when the virtuous pretend to do evil but actually do good. Thus the devil tests their virtue and their virtue tests heaven.

IV. i. 21–22. *'As doth the ... Boding to all'* = As the raven, perching on a house of disease, indicates that all within are doomed.

IV. i. 25–29. *'as knaves be ... they must blab'* = there are men who, through their efforts at seduction or by affection for a mistress, once they have sex they can't refrain from talking about it.

IV. i. 63. *'horned man'* = a cuckolded man (reputed to grow horns).

IV. i. 67–70. *'Think every bearded ... dare swear peculiar'* = Consider that every married man is in the same situation as you. Millions of people commit adultery every night and all think their situation is unique.

IV. i. 77. *'here o'erwhelmed'*; Q. 1, 'here ere while, mad'.

IV. i. 80. *'And laid good 'scuse upon your ecstasy'* = And made good excuses for your incapacitation.

IV. i. 105–106. *'The worser that ... even kills me.'* = I feel worse that you address me by the title that I have so painfully lost.

IV. i. 122. (*'What, a customer!'*); ii. 73–76; iii. 60–63, 87–104; omitted in Q. 1.

IV. i. 122–124. *'I prithee, bear ... so unwholesome.'* = Please give my intelligence some credit; don't think that it is sick.

IV. i. 139–140. *'and, by this hand, she falls me'*; so Collier; Q. 1, reads *'by this hand she fals'*; Ff., *'and falls me'*; Qq. 2, 3, *'fals me'*.

IV. i. 166–168. *'An you'll come ... next prepared for'* = If you come to supper tonight, that's fine by me. If not, come when you are ready.

IV. i. 188. *'I would have ... years a-killing'* = I would spend nine years killing him.

IV. i. 208–210. *'If you are ... comes near nobody'* = If you like her sinning, then give her licence to sin, because if it doesn't affect you, it doesn't affect anyone else.

IV. i. 248. *'Deputing Cassio in his government'* = Appointing Cassio as his deputy.

IV. i. 256–257. *'If that the ... prove a crocodile.'* Othello alludes to the belief that crocodiles shed tears to disarm and attract their victims.

IV. i. 274. *'Goats and monkeys!'* These two animals were associated with promiscuity.

IV. i. 276. *'This the nature,'* Pope's reading; Qq., *'This the noble nature'*; Ff. *'Is this the nature.'*

IV. i. 281–283. *'I may not ... heaven he were!'* = I am afraid to say what he has become, but if Othello isn't sound of mind, I wish he were.

IV. ii. 16. *'Let heaven requite ... the serpent's curse!'* = May heaven punish them with the curse of the snake that tempted Adam and Eve.

IV. ii. 18–19. *'the purest of ... foul as slander'* = [If Desdemona is unfaithful] then even the most faithful wife can be slandered as corrupt.

IV. ii. 27. *'Some of your function, mistress'*. Othello is essentially saying that Desdemona is a brothel-keeper, and should do her job as such.

IV. ii. 53–55. *'but, alas, to ... unmoving finger at!'* = It will make me a permanent object of mockery, sitting under the slow hand of time.

IV. ii. 66–67. *'O, ay; as ... even with blowing'* = O, yes, as the flies in the abattoir breed on the rotting carcasses.

IV. ii. 104. *'But what should go by water'* = But what should be said in tears.

IV. ii. 108–109. *'How have I ... my least misuse?'* = What have I done that he should judge the smallest fault as the lowest sin?

IV. ii. 109. *'least misuse'*; Q. 1, *'greatest abuse'*; Collier MS., *'least misdeede'*.

IV. ii. 146. *'That turn'd your ... seamy side without'* = That turned your intelligence inside out.

IV. ii. 157–158. *'though he do ... To beggarly divorcement'* = even though he casts me out to live in poverty.

IV. ii. 170. *'The messengers of Venice stay the meat'*; Knight's reading; F. 1, *'The Messengers of Venice staies the meate'*; Ff. 2, 3, 4, *'The Messenger of Venice staies the meate'*; Q. 1, *'And the great Messengers of Venice stay'*; Qq. 2, 3, *'The meate, great Messengers of Venice stay.'*

IV. ii. 208–209. *'from this instant ... than ever before'* = I now have a new-found respect for you.

IV. ii. 220–222. *'take me from ... for my life'* = betray me so I leave this world and devise war machines for killing me.

IV. ii. 232–233. *'none can be so ... removing of Cassio.'* = Nothing can be so effective as the removal of Cassio.

IV. iii. 23. *'All's one. Good faith'*; Q. 1, *'All's one good faith'*; Qq. 2, 3, *'All's one; good father'*; Ff., *'All's one: good Father.'*

IV. iii. 26. *'Barbara'*; Qq. read *'Barbary'*; F. 1, *'Barbarie'*.

IV. iii. 41, &c; the original of Desdemona's song is to be found in Percy's *Reliques* under the title of *'A Lover's Complaint, being forsaken of his Love'*, where the plaintive lover is a man.

IV. iii. 41. *'sighing'*; Ff., *'singing'*; Q. 3, *'singhing'*; F. 1 (Dev.) *'sining'*.

IV. iii. 80. *'Why, the wrong ... i' the world'* = The offence is only an offence in public opinion.

IV. iii. 85–86. *'and as many ... they played for'* = and as many additional people who would populate the world they were playing for.

IV. iii. 89. *'And pour our treasures into foreign laps'* = And give the sexual pleasures due to us to other women.

IV. iii. 104. *'The ills we ... instruct us so.'* = We have learned our transgressions from those of men.

IV. iii. 105–106. *'heaven me such ... by bad mend!'* = Heaven grant that I take moral lessons from my cruel experiences and not imitate them.

V. i. 2. *'Wear thy good rapier bare, and put it home'* = Have your sword ready [i.e. out of its scabbard] and push it in deep.

V. i. 4. *'It makes us, or it mars us'* = It will either bring us victory or destroy us.

V. i. 26. *'I will make proof of thine'* = I will test how protective is your coat.

V. i. 35. *'Forth of my ... eyes, are blotted'* = I have removed the spell cast over me by your eyes.

V. i. 66. *'As you shall prove us, praise us'* = Praise us if you think we are worthy.

V. i. 82–83; ii. 82, 185–193, 266–272; omitted in Q. 1.

V. i. 93–95. *'cry you gentle ... so neglected you'* = Forgive me, but the crisis unfolding before me has distracted me from the good manners you deserve.

V. i. 101. *'Save you your labour'* = You are wasting your efforts.

V. i. 105. *'gentlemen'*, the reading of Ff.; Qq., *'Gentlewoman'*.

V. i. 107. *'if you stare'*; so Ff.; Qq. 1, 2, *'an you stirre'*; Q. 3, *'an you stirr'*; Anon conj. *'if you stay'*.

V. i. 110. *'Though tongues were out of use'* = Though nothing was being said.

V. i. 119. *'but I therefore shake not'* = but I am not scared.

V. i. 129. *'fordoes me quite'* = destroys my peace completely.

V. ii. 1. *'It is the cause, it is the cause'* = It is the offence... Othello is alluding to the fact that adultery is compelling him to act.

V. ii. 7. *'Put out the light, and then put out the light'*; i.e. 'put out the light, and then put out the light of life.' The Cambridge Editors give some dozen variant methods of punctuating and reading the line, but it is perfectly clear as it stands.

V. ii. 8. *'thou flaming minister'* = the guiding light of a torch.

V. ii. 11. *'Thou cunning'st pattern of excelling nature'* = You most magnificent but cunning work of nature.

V. ii. 19–20. *'one more, and ... ne'er so fatal'* = one more kiss, so sweet but yet so deadly.

V. ii. 27–28. *'Unreconciled as yet ... for it straight'* = If you have not yet confessed a crime to heaven for forgiveness, do it immediately.

V. ii. 40. *'They are loves I bear to you'* = All my sins are acts of love to you.

V. ii. 60–61. *'But with such ... gave him token'* = But only with the general love of humanity sanctioned by God; I never gave him a gift of romantic love.

V. ii. 64–65. *'And makest me ... thought a sacrifice'* = If you stick with your claims of innocence, then what I am about to do is murder, not a sacrifice.

V. ii. 71. *'his mouth is stopp'd'* = He has been killed.

V. ii. 74–75. *'Had all his ... for them all'* = If he had as many lives as the hairs on his head, my desire for revenge had the capacity to kill them all.

V. ii. 100–101. *'that the affrighted ... yawn at alteration'* = the shocked planet would gape, open-mouthed, at this reworking of its plan.

V. ii. 115–116. *'then murder's out ... revenge grows harsh'* = then the murder I have committed has gone wrong and my revenge brings no satisfaction.

V. ii. 134. *'She was false as water'.* The implication is that water's flow is unpredictable and uncontrollable.

V. ii. 151. *'made mocks with love'*; 'taken advantage to play upon the weakness of passion' (Johnson).

V. ii. 157. *'She was too fond of her most filthy bargain'.* She was too devoted to the destructive marriage.

V. ii. 161. *'Peace, you were best'* = You had better be silent.

V. ii. 172. *'Disprove this villain'*; Capell, *'Disprove it, villain.'*

V. ii. 196. *''Tis proper I obey him, but not now'* = Custom says I should be obedient, but now is not the time.

V. ii. 213. *'And she did gratify his amorous works'* = She gave in to his lust.

V. ii. 220. *'as liberal as the north'* = as freely as the north wind blows.

V. ii. 234–235. *'Are there no ... for the thunder?'* = Are the stones in heaven only used to make thunder [and not to kill villains]?

V. ii. 243–244. *'I am not ... gets my sword'* = I lack valour, and now every weakling can take my sword.

V. ii. 247–248. *'I will play ... die in music'.* A reference to Greek mythology, in which the swan is reputed to sing beautifully at the point of death.

V. ii. 323. *'Which wrought to his desire'* = Which played into his hands.

V. ii. 327. *'That I was cast'* = For which I was dismissed.

V. ii. 333–335. *'If there be ... shall be his'* = If there are any ingenious torture methods that can inflict the worst pain while keeping him alive, inflict them on him.

V. ii. 337. *'bring away'*; Qq., *'bring him away'*; Collier MS., *'bring them away'*.

V. ii. 347–348. *'Like the base ... all his tribe'* = Like the uncivilized Indian who does not recognize an object of precious value. The Folio has 'Judean' in place of 'Indian', interpreted to refer to the betrayer of Christ, Judas Iscariot, who threw away 'the pearl' of the Kingdom of Heaven.

WILLIAM SHAKESPEARE – HIS LIFE AND TIMES

We have few details of Shakespeare's personal life, and some of these are disputed, but we can trace his life in theatre with some confidence. This was a man who learned his craft; insisted on fair remuneration; found (and retained) royal favour and escaped political snares. Aligned with one company, he could write with specific actors in mind and experiment as different theatres offered new staging possibilities. His creativity was impacted only by frequent outbreaks of plague, which closed the theatres.

1557

John Shakespeare marries Mary Arden. The couple may have known each other since childhood; his father farmed land owned by her father.

26 APRIL 1564

The couple's third child, William, is baptized. His date of birth is not known, and the day usually celebrated – 23 April, or Saint George's Day – appeals only because this is known to be the day of his death, in 1616. That said, baptism was expected during this period to take place no later than seven days after birth.

EDUCATION

William is probably educated at the King's New School in Stratford-upon-Avon, about a quarter-mile from his home.

At this time, a grammar school education involves principally the teaching of Latin (with some Greek), preparing boys for careers in the civil service. The art of rhetoric teaches them how to communicate with an audience, learning the importance of delivery and gesture.

Boys also study classical poetry and drama, and write their own compositions, in both English and Latin or Greek. They perform these in front of their class – and sometimes perform plays on holidays.

JULY 1575, KENILWORTH

The Earl of Leicester's Men, a major acting company, perform *The Delivery of the Lady of the Lake* at Kenilworth Castle. Crowds flock to their performances, from 9 to 27 July, and it is possible that William is among them. A reference to 'Arion on the dolphin's back' in *Twelfth Night* (I. ii. 15) may reflect his familiarity with the classical tale, but it may also echo a particularly noteworthy spectacle: musicians performing inside a dolphin.

27 NOVEMBER 1582

A marriage licence is issued to William, then aged 18, and Anne Hathaway, then aged 26. It's probable the marriage is one of necessity: permission is granted to read the marriage banns only once (not the usual three times) and a daughter, Susanna, is baptized less than six months later, on 26 May 1583.

2 FEBRUARY 1585

Twins, son Hamnet and daughter Judith, are baptized.

1585–1592, THE 'LOST YEARS'

William disappears from the historical record, and we do not know how he supports his young family during this time. Is he a schoolmaster? A legal clerk? A soldier?

At some point in the late 1880s, he arrives in London. Perhaps to avoid prosecution for poaching deer – though probably not. This and other stories arise in the years (and centuries) following his death, in part a response to misreading contemporary documents. 'Shakespeare' is a common enough name in the sixteenth century, and there is only one document that seems certain to refer to William: a 'complaints bill' for a case before the Queen's Bench between 1588 and 1589.

SHAKESPEARE, THE ACTOR

William begins his life in the theatre as an actor. This aspect of his life is often overlooked, not least because actors are held in low esteem during his lifetime – and, indeed, for many centuries after it.

Reform of the Poor Laws during Elizabeth's reign had made life for travelling companies particularly difficult. An act 'for the punishment of vagabondes' (1572) allowed for the arrest and imprisonment of the unemployed, and itinerant actors were often targeted. Acting companies therefore required the protection of theatrical sponsors such as the Earl of Leicester and the Earl of Sussex, whose playing company the young William joins.

Though never a star, he will act for 15 years – which suggests a certain skill. At a time when audiences are both loud and generous with their responses, a bad player will be hissed from the stage, their exit further encouraged by the lobbing of an orange or two. His first biographer, Nicolas Rowe, tells us that his role as the Ghost in *Hamlet* was 'the top of his performance'. William also appears in the cast list for several plays by Ben Jonson, including *Sejanus*, performed in 1603.

1589–1592, EARLY WRITING

Apparently recognizing that he does not excel as an actor, William finds a new role: he breathes new life into old and tired plays, collaborates with established dramatists and begins to write alone.

With others, he writes: *The Second Part of Henry the Sixth* (1591); *The Third Part of Henry the Sixth* (1591); *The Lamentable Tragedy of Titus Andronicus* (1592); and *The First Part of Henry the Sixth* (1592).

On his own, he writes the following plays (whose dates are difficult to establish with any certainty): *The Taming of the Shrew* (1589–1592); *The Two Gentleman of Verona* (1591–1592); and *King Richard the Third* (1592/4). Lord Strange's Men are associated with the first performance of this last play, and Lord Strange himself is a direct descendant of Thomas Stanley, a character in the play whose role is pivotal. William may be a member of the company.

1592, 'AN UPSTART CROW'

Robert Greene, a popular dramatist, publishes a pamphlet, *Greenes, Groats-worth of Witte, bought with a million of Repentance*. He has both a BA and an MA from Cambridge, and complains:

> there is an upstart Crow, beautified with our feathers, that with his Tygers hart wrapt in a Players hyde, supposes he is as well able to bombast out a blanke verse as the best of you: and being an absolute Johannes fac totum, is in his owne conceit the onely Shake-scene in a countrey.

This *Johannes fac totum* is a Jack of all trades – and, obviously, a master of none. Drama should clearly be left to university graduates, not actors.

Just six years later, however, another Cambridge graduate, the author Francis Meres, will write:

> As Plautus and Seneca are accounted the best for comedy and tragedy among the Latins, so Shakespeare among the English is the most excellent in both kinds for the stage.

Incidentally, the reference to 'his Tygers hart wrapt in a Players hyde' is an allusion to a line from *Henry VI, Part III* – which suggests the play had enjoyed considerable success.

1593–1594

Plague closes the theatres, and Lord Strange's Men leave London to tour. William writes two narrative poems, which prove popular and will be reprinted several times during his lifetime. He dedicates both to Henry Wriothesley, 3rd Earl of Southampton. The dedication for Venus and Adonis is brief – 'The love I dedicate to your Lordship is without end'; the dedication for *The Rape of Lucrèce* is extravagant:

> The love I dedicate to your lordship is without end ... What I have done is yours; what I have to do is yours; being part in all I have, devoted yours.

We do not know the nature of the relationship between the two men, and both dedications offer few clues – during this period, writers depend on their sponsors for support, political as well as financial. However, the Earl is often identified as the 'Fair Youth' of Shakespeare's sonnets: his celebrated looks and personality seem to match.

It's an identification that is disputed, not least because Henry is 39 (hardly a youth) when the sonnets are first published, in 1609 – though this is a collection written between 1593 and 1608.

1594, *THE COMEDY OF ERRORS*

William adapts *Menaechmi*, by Plautus – a play he may well have read at school. It is performed by 'a company of base and common fellows' at Gray's Inn Hall on 28 December 1594.

1594, THE LORD CHAMBERLAIN'S MEN

Many members of Lord Strange's Men leave to found this 'playing company', under the patronage of Henry Carey, 1st Baron Hunsdon and the Lord Chamberlain. It will become known as the King's Men in 1603, when the new king, James I, becomes patron.

Profits (and debts) are split between eight 'sharers', including William and Richard Burbage, who will become one of the most famous actors of his time and the first to play the roles of Hamlet, Othello, King Lear and Macbeth.

With this new arrangement, William effectively receives royalties for his work, at a time when writers are usually at the mercy of theatre managers, earning low prices and paid only according to the amount produced. In 1600, the impresario Philip Henslowe is paying £6–7 a play and the proceeds from one day's performance.

Originally the company performs at The Theatre, Shoreditch. On 29 December 1598, after difficulties with the landlord and a move to another theatre, The Theatre is dismantled overnight and carried south of the river to Southwark, where a new theatre is built: The Globe.

1595–1596

The Lord Chamberlain's Men have exclusive rights to perform William's plays, which gives him an unusual opportunity – to develop roles for and in collaboration with the actors.

• *Love's Labour's Lost*
Probably written around this time, the play is unusual for having no clear literary source while its pageants recall royal entertainments. (It will be performed in front of the Queen at Christmas, 1597.)
Does the play have a sequel, *Love's Labour's Won*? Francis Meres suggests as much, but it's not certain whether this is a play that has now been lost or is simply an alternative title to another play.

• *A Midsummer Night's Dream*
This may be the first play William writes for the Lord Chamberlain's Men – though the first certain date we have for its performance is 1604 at Hampton Court. Bottom may have been played by the great comic actor Will Kempe.

• *The Tragedy of Romeo and Juliet*
According to the First Quarto, published in 1597, this play 'hath been often (and with great applause) plaid publiquely' – which suggests it is an immediate success. Richard Burbage probably plays Romeo, and a misprint in the First Quarto suggests that Will Kempe plays Peter.

• *The Life and Death of King Richard the Second*
It's possible that William plays the role of John of Gaunt. The play is popular and will be printed three times by 1598.

11 AUGUST 1596

Son Hamnet is buried, dead from unknown causes at the age of 11.

1597–1598

Throughout his career, William moves between London and Stratford, where he buys New Place as his family home, in 1597. It is one of the largest properties in the town, which suggests he has enjoyed considerable financial success.

By 1598, he has also secured a reputation: his name is now a selling point and appears on the title pages of editions of his plays.

• *The Merchant of Venice*
Richard Burbage plays Shylock and Will Kempe plays Lancelot Gobbo, in a play described by Francis Meres and the First Folio as a comedy. It has been performed 'divers times' by 1600, the date of a first edition.

• *The First Part of Henry the Fourth*
The character we know now as Falstaff is originally called Oldcastle. This proves controversial: Oldcastle's descendants, the Lords Cobham, are powerful and take advantage when Henry Carey, the Lord Chamberlain, dies. The company is now 'piteously persecuted by the Lord Mayor and the aldermen', according to the contemporary playwright Thomas Nashe. Within the year, the appointment of Carey's son to Lord Chamberlain restores the company's protection, and Oldcastle is renamed Falstaff.

• *The Second Part of Henry the Fourth*
The epilogue thanks the audience and assures them that Sir John Falstaff will return in a new play. It also clarifies that Falstaff is not Oldcastle, who 'died martyr, and this is not the man'.

• *Much Ado About Nothing*
The most performed of Shakespeare's comedies, it is very popular in the years following its first performance. Will Kempe plays Dogberry, who will leave the company in 1599 – possibly because his talent for improvisation proves irritating. *Hamlet* (written within the next two years) includes this advice to the Players: 'And let those that play your clowns speak no more than is set down for them'.

1599

• *The Life of Henry the Fifth*
In the final act, Henry's triumphant return from London is compared to the Earl of Essex, soon to be 'from Ireland coming, / Bringing rebellion broached on his sword'. It's a confident prediction for the Queen's favourite, but by June England knows that his expedition has failed: the new play is already out of date.

• *As You Like It*
Scholars agree that this is the first play to be performed at the
Globe. Tradition has it that William plays Adam, who may have
written the role of Rosalind with a specific boy player in mind.

• *The Tragedy of Julius Caesar*
Richard Burbage plays the role of Brutus. Caesar is played by the
actor John Heminges, who will be co-editor of the First Folio.

1600–1601

• *The Tragedy of Hamlet*
Richard Burbage is the first to play the Prince. Many believe that
John Heminges plays Polonius, and that contemporary audiences
laugh at the boastful line: 'I did enact Julius Caesar: I was killed i'
the Capitol; Brutus killed me'.

• *The Merry Wives of Windsor*
A play that shows signs of having been written in haste.
Biographer Nicolas Rowe insists that the Queen 'was so well
pleased with that admirable character of *Falstaff*, in the two parts
of *Henry the Fourth*, that she commanded him [Shakespeare] to
continue it for one play more, and to shew him in love'. It's a
story that has as many detractors as supporters.

• *Twelfth Night, or What You Will*
Whether or not this is commissioned to perform during Twelfth
Night celebrations at Whitehall Palace in 1601, the comedy is
written around this time. Robert Arnim has replaced Will Kempe as
the leading comic actor, and William is now writing for him: Feste
is a character who is no mere entertainer but shows a keen
intelligence.

1603–1610

Repeated outbreaks of plague close theatres (for a total of 60 months
– five full years), and William's output slows.

He collaborates several times with Thomas Middleton, who also
contributes scenes to Macbeth, and with George Wilkins for *Pericles,
Prince of Tyre* (1608). The Tragedy of Cymbeline (1610) also shows
signs of collaboration.

In Thomas North's translation of *Plutarch's Lives* (first published in
1580, then expanded in 1595 and again in 1603), he finds inspiration for
The Tragedy of Antony and Cleopatra (1607–1608) and *Coriolanus*
(1605–1608). It's clear he also reads Plutarch's original Greek text closely.

There are no records of performances for *All's Well That Ends Well* (1605) or *The Life of Timon of Athens* (1605), which may never have been produced.

• *The Tragedy of Othello* (1604)
Richard Burbage plays the Moor. It is possible that Robert Arnim plays Iago: he was the actor most usually given songs, and Iago sings two drinking songs. The historical setting – the Turkish invasion of Cyprus, leading to the Battle of Lepanto – may be politically astute: a new monarch sits on the throne, James I, and he has recently written a poem about the battle.

• *Measure for Measure* (1604)
This may have been prompted by his research for Othello: an important source for both plays is Cinthio's Gli Hecatommithi.

• *The Tragedy of King Lear* (1605–1606)
Richard Arnim plays the Fool, a character who is no clown but who dares to criticize the king even as he remains loyal. Richard Burbage plays Lear, a story with contemporary echoes. In 1603, Sir Brian Annesley, a rich father of three daughters, had become senile. His two older daughters tried to take advantage to contest his will, knowing that his main beneficiary was their younger sister, Cordell.

• *The Tragedy of Macbeth* (1606)
Several details suggest strongly that this play was written in the aftermath of the Gunpowder Plot of 1605. The words 'fair' and 'foul' are the echoes of a sermon given by Lancelot Andrewes in front of the king; a medal struck to celebrate the plot's thwarting depicted a serpent hiding among flowers, echoing the advice given by Lady Macbeth: 'Look like the innocent flower, but be the serpent under't'.

1611

• *The Winter's Tale*
The play is based closely on *Pandosto*, by Robert Greene who had been so contemptuous of the 'upstart crow'. Staged at the Globe – the earliest performance recorded is May – it will be performed at Court in front of the King in November.

• *The Tempest*
This seems to have been written for staging at the Blackfriars playhouse, an indoor theatre owned by the company since 1608.

The characters who leave the stage at the end of Act IV are the same who return for Act V. This suggests an interval – probably to replace the candles and torches that provided lighting.

1612–1614

William now works with John Fletcher, who will eventually replace him as the company's playwright.

23 APRIL 1616

William dies. The cause is unknown and seems to have been unexpected; he had declared himself to be in 'perfect health' when preparing his will, barely a month earlier. Half a century later, John Ward, vicar of Stratford, will record the local gossip: 'Shakespeare, Drayton, and Ben Jonson had a merry meeting and, it seems, drank too hard, for Shakespeare died of a fever there contracted.'

Three King's Men receive bequests: Richard Burbage, John Heminges and Henry Condell.

13 MARCH 1619

Richard Burbage dies – and London mourns. 'He's gone and with him what a world are dead,' writes an anonymous poet, remembering 'Hamlet ... scant of breath', 'Tyrant Macbeth with unwash'd, bloody hand', and 'let me not forget one chiefest part, / Wherein, beyond the rest, he mov'd the heart; / The grieved Moor'.

1623, THE FIRST FOLIO

John Heminges and his fellow King's Man Henry Condell prepare and edit *Mr. William Shakespeare's Comedies, Histories, & Tragedies* for publication. Its significance cannot be underestimated: it is the only reliable text for about 20 plays, and the first publication for a further 18.

The preface tells us that a funerary monument has been erected at Holy Trinity Church, Stratford to honour William Shakespeare, a poet with the genius of Socrates and the art of Virgil: 'The earth buries him, the people mourn him, [Mount] Olympus possesses him'.